Why I am not a Policeman ?

James Vadackumchery

2001
Kaveri Books
New Delhi-110002

First Published in 2001
ISBN 81-7479-042-X

Published by : Rakesh Goel
Kaveri Books
4697/5-21A, Ansari Road
New Delhi-110 002 (India).

Tel. : 328 8140, 324 5799
Fax : 011-719 9029
E-mail : kaveribooks@vsnl.com

Laser Typesetting by : Aarati Computers, Delhi-110 009

Printed at : Chawla Offset Printers, Delhi-110 052

PRINTD IN INDIA

----❖-❖-❖----

I dedicate this book to

Rev. Kuriakose

Rev. Mary Louvisa

Rev. Mary Jane

Chakkappen, Mariamma

Michael, Brigitta

Shelsy, Rajan

Osborn, Mary

Alphonsa, Mathew

Valsa, Francis

Cleatus, Anitha

Philo, George

Litty, Jomy on the eve of the second millennium and to Mary, Neethu and Neethie on the dawn of the third millennium.

----❖-❖-❖----

Contents

Contents

Preface

Lord Bertrand Russel wrote "*Why I am not a Christian*" and I read the book in 1969 when I was doing a course in Philosophy and Humanities. It was a book edited by Professor Paul Edwards of New York University and the editor had contributed a full account of the highly controversial "Bertrand Russel Case" of 1940, in which Russel was judicially declared "unfit' to teach philosophy. The account given by the editor impressed me a lot and after thirty years, I wish to author a title "Why I am not a Policeman?". Before anything else I write, I quote Russell himself: "The world needs open hearts and open minds, and it is not through rigid systems, whether old or new, that these can be derived".

After passing M.A. in Criminology and Forensic Science and a LL.B. degree with high first class, gold medal and rank in order of merit from the University of Saugor (as the University then was known), I got admission to do M.Phil course in Melbourne University, Australia. I met Mr. V.N. Rajan, then Inspector General of Police, Kerala State and told him that I preferred to do a job in Kerala Police. According to the recommendations of the Central Committee on Police Training, instituted by Government of India, Kerala Police wanted to get the services of a teacher qualified in criminology to give instructions to the officer trainees at the Police Training College, Thiruvananthapuram. Mr. V.M. Rajan told me that I should send my bio-data along with a request to appoint me as a deputy superintendent of police to teach criminology. I decided to do so and I got a letter appointing me as criminologist on contract basis for nine months or so. I felt sorry for not appointing me as a deputy superintendent of police. I started working as a civilian, criminologist by designation, on the faculty of the Police Training College, Thiruvananthapuram.

After a few months of service at the police training college, I understood that I could work as a civilian in police rather than wearing a police uniform. I discussed my desire with Dr. P.J. Alexander, the then deputy inspector general of police, (training) and he advised me that I should not opt for a police job. He had many reasons for the same and one most important reason was that I would not be free in my thoughts and expressions if I wore a police garb. I thank Dr. P.J. Alexander for his advice and from then and till now, I never wished to become a policeman. Police is a noble profession and only those who are called specially to peform such functions can take up the challenge. People who have received adequate human formation and who possess an upright conscience can enviably become policemen. I do not think that I have the special vocation to become a policeman. I notice just infront of me some people who lack adequate human formation and upright human conscience infiltrating into police service and they attempt to make the service a muscle power to earn many things to their favour. Consequently, they do not behave with a sense of just justice in their transactions. When the sense of just justice is lost, the sense human approach is also threatened and poisoned, as I may emphatically say, 'without the sense of just justice, the policeman is not behaving like a man and precisely therefore, his actions become unintelligible. Policeman then is no longer able to see himself as a public servant different from a person who does things for his own benefits. He regards himself then as a person who wants to earn as much as he can from the jobs he does. People then consider him as an earthly creature which is clothed in khaki uniform and who no longer grasps the sublime character of police service to people. He no longer considers his job as something "noble" entrusted to his responsibility by the people. Police job and duty he considers as something he can control and manipulate for his advantage.

When a judge in Allahabad said that the police in India is an organized group of criminals, no one except the police administration got wild at the pronouncement. They went with an appeal to the Supreme Court and got that portion of the judgement expunched. Yet, the Apex Court reaffirmed that there was a lot of truth behind that exaggerated version of the learned judge in Allahabad. When Amnesty International reported that torture had been institutionalized in police and custodial deaths were many in police lockups, we dismissed the statement by saying that it was an interference to the internal affairs of the Country. Going back still further to the 19th century, Torture Commission categorically stated that torture was in vogue in the erstwhile Madras Presidency. Amidst all these observations and adverse comments against the police, policemen are killed on duty and become martyrs on the altar of police service to people and the number has been going up year after year. How many of them belong to the civil police? That is not asked by many; yet these good works rendered by the police make the service meaningful and commendable. Perhaps, that is the precise reason why the service is retained by the people amidst unpalatable criticisms against the police.

'Why I am a policeman?' — this question needs an answer now and an answer to the question will be "to render human services in a human rights friendly way". In rendering human services, the police may have to use force not as means or weapon to annihilate the people, but to offer services to the people so that they continue to live in peace and harmony. Somehow or other, this noble concept was not inculcated to Indian police by the British and therefore, the police continued to function as a deterrent force even after India became independent. But, today, owing to a change in outlook and attitude and perhaps thanks to public demands and social compulsions, the police are showing an inclination to be more people friendly in their attitudes and approaches. Third millennium police, it is hoped or almost confirmed, will be people's police asserting the principle that the police are the people and the people are the police.

My life in police has helped me to understand policemen/ officers in close quarters. I could learn that many have wrong concepts about crime, causes of crime, remedial measures etc.. Nevertheless, they are not prepared to accept the same. Conflicts arise between ignorance and the reluctance to accept the ignorance. Some use their authority, authoritarian ego and exercise of pseudo-authority to compensate the mental conflicts they have. Some police officers/men have wrong concepts about the role of police in a democracy, but they are not prepared to accept their ignorance. There was a time when people accepted even "*ignorance*" as "*knowledge*" and if *ignorance* comes from a police officer/man, certainly, people accepted it as knowledge or even as wisdom even when they knew that the police officer/man spoke non-sense. Time has changed and the people are not prepared to accept ignorance as knowledge, no matter the ignorance comes from any ranks in police. I am a policeman because I know what I am and what I ought to be. How many police personnel can say so boldly?

Many people have asked me : "what are you in police?". "Are you a head-constable?" — ask some villagers who think that a head constable is an important person in police. Of course, a head constable is important. He manages many things as the people have more contacts with the head constable at the station house level than the director general of police at the police headquarters. Some other people ask me: "are you the inspector general of police?"and to them I used to ask a counter question: "What do you think about me?". Many of them have said: "you don't look like a policeman". Yes, the policeman/officer has a look, a style of walk, a method of talk and a sort of language which perhaps I do not have. A professional look, talk, walk and language may be different in a criminologist-different from the same of a policeman/officer. Between the two, I liked the former although my close association with policemen/officers might have made me too to behave like a policeman/officer at times unconsciously although I have consciously tried in many ways not to exhibit police *personality traits* when I interacted with people. Any behaviour, not accepted by the dominant culture-let it come from the highest authority — will be resented against atleast in silent language or body behaviour. If it comes from the police authority, certainly that too is reacted against and in a democracy, the reactions may be open or explicit. Once a policeman uttered "bastard" and later the one who heard the epithet commented: "he was addressing himself by that epithet" and the behaviour was unfavourably commented against the whole department. I am a policeman and therefore I ought to be a policeman-and the policeman, I mean must be a policeman with desirable personality traits. This thinking must dominate the policeman in a democracy. Any undesirable behaviour is harmful not only for the one who behaves in that way, but also to the organization he represents. Any behaviour has short-run and long-run effects. An undesirable behaviour may have an immediate advantage, but may also have a great disadvantage in the long run.

This is a time of revival for police. After the advent of human rights consciousness and acceptance of transparency and accountability in police work, the police have become more conscious of their responsibility to the public than what it was earlier. A number of well established non-governmental organizations, public interest litigation societies, the press, media and well meaning citizens keep a watch and constant vigil on police activities. As a result, the temper of the policeman has become much more tolerant to people and the watch-men of police activities have less hesitation to openly criiticize the police everywhere—sometimes with justifications and at other times without justifications. In India, vulgar anti-police propaganda is rampant and the more aggressive anti-police propagandists go to any extent to interpret many things done by police to be anti-people or anti-democratic. This is of bad taste and it makes the police to be less active in their work. Every man in public is a policeman and therefore each one must ask the question to himself: "Why cann't I be a policeman?". Think of an issue from the point of view of the policeman, then one may see that the policeman has many justifications for what he does. It is argued that iron bars are given to the lockup doors in police stations for the detinue to count and recount them when he has nothing to do in the custodial facility. It is true that he counts and recounts the bars when he is inside the police lockup. But I don't think that a policeman will agree with the argument. The iron bars are given to the doors so that the policeman can see what does the detainee do inside the lockup. If he makes an attempt to commit suicide, the policeman can stop it if iron bars are given.

The policeman may as well argue that a detinue may be kept with short loin clothes or only with undergarments inside a police lock-up as a precaution against suicidal attempts by the detainee. I can not think that the general public and the detinues themselves will agree with the arguments. They may say that the clothes one wears have never become a cause of suicides, although it may be used as a means to commit suicide. The real cause of custodial suicides must be searched elsewhere and therefore the general public argue that keeping a detinue in nakedness or half-nakedness in police lockups is a human right violation. The law says that the detinue in police lockup must be provided with necessary wearing apparel and the necessary wearing apparel in a given society is decided by the culture prevailing in society and not at all by the policeman who takes a decision by his subjective scales. It may mean that there should not be conflicts between the policeman and the man on the street-the ordinary man-whenever a policeman takes a decision for enforcing it on others who are, more often than not, helpless and forsaken in police lockups.

There exists the story of a thief in a police aid-post. The story is as under: The superintendent of police once made a visit to a police aid-post and the intention was to conduct a surprise inspection. He found a thief on the corner of a room and also a police hat on the table in the room. The policeman was not found anywhere. He made a search for the policeman and he learnt that he has gone to catch another thief. The story took place at a time when a police cap/hat could deter the people and the thieves, but the situation has changed now. Even pistols and .303 rifles can not deter the people now. The thinking today is that the hat, cap, uniform,whistle, boots, rifles, pistols, lathies, canes, training etc..are intended to offer service to people and not to cause deterrence among them. "Deter the people and rule"-approach may not yield good dividends in a democracy and the principle is equally applicable in democracy's police as well. Older policemen narrate a lot of police stories and police adventures and the listeners to such so called "adventures" feel boring to hear them and make comments, "*Indecent, bad, unethical, intolerable, undemocratic, cruel, barbarous etc*...and perhaps such behavioural patterns shown by yesterday's policemen have caricatured the police image in the present day society. Whatever that be, there is no meaning in crying over the spilt milk or cursing the past. Today's policeman ought to be different from what he was in the past. "Why I am a policeman?" — and the answer to the question should be: "I am a policeman because I want to be human rights friendly and I can be". The old police stories and the old policemen/officers are not to be taken as models, if they teach perverted ideas and wrong examples. The *old* is not always gold and some of the old things must be buried and the burying process is going on now.

One thing alone is certain in government service and that there is the day of retirement. Every success leads but to one's retirement from service. On retirement one must feel that his service was praise worthy. If one must feel so, he must be honest and just in his thoughts, words and actions. One must be considerate to others and compassionate to the people entrusted to his responsible concern and care. True compassion leads to sharing another's pain and another here means all including the suspects in police custody. No society or victim of offence may desire to do injustice to the crime-doers as it is never licit to commit a crime to prove a crime. How many people might have been killed in police custody, might have committed suicide, might have been tortured, might have been harassed, might have been humiliated? There is no accurate account of the figures, yet one may well guess about it. Some policemen tell that they want to rectify the mistakes committed by their predecessors who had wrong notions of policing a democracy. Police are the friends of the people and they continue to be so in the years to come. If the police are not able to do so, then there is no meaning in telling that the police are public servants who want to be the friends of the people. In police work, the people are at the centre and everything done by police must be for the people. Every law is made for man and every public servant is expected to enforce the law for the people and their welfare. The policemen must accept this reality and tune their functions accordingly. Police in the past could not understand their responsibility in this regard. They accused the British for their defects even after India became independent. I met a British police officer in a seminar and he told me that the blaming of the British for the misbehaviour shown by the Indian Police after 50 years of freedom should be stopped. Any attempt to blame the British still is a conscious effort to evade the responsibility for what the police do here and now. I have written this earlier in one of my books and I reiterate it here because it was a moment I was silenced by the British police officer. "*Why I am a policeman?*"–he said–"*should be asked by every Indian policeman and he must answer the question expressing his desire to become an Indian Policeman, and not a policeman of the British past, in a democracy*". Yes. There is a point in that, for every policeman does not think always that he is an Indian policeman of the democracy. Police job is characterized by dignity and surrounded by responsibilities. Policemen themselves must accept this principle first and then only they will have a self esteem in themselves and a sense of respect for others. Policeman is not the absolute master and final judge of everything he does for the people in a democracy-rather, he is the servant of the people to do things in the way the people in their corporate capacity want him to do.

Police functions are important because they involve many duties which people individually can not do. In performing the duties thus entrusted to police, they have to take into account the common good of man. If the use of only minimum force is sufficient to defend the life and property of people against an aggressor and to protect public order and the harmonious living of people, the police must limit themselves to such minimum force, for it better corresponds to the expectations of the people and is more in conformity to the dignity of human person. When a policeman asks to himself "*Why I am a Policeman?*", he must see before himself the weak and the defenceless before he initiates any action. The weak and the defenceless human beings find the policeman as their defence against the arrogance and caprice of the strong and the unjust in society. The deliberate neglect of the weak and the deliberate protection offered to the strong and the unjust are evils and can never be justified either as an end in itself or as a means to any good end. If media reports are true, some policemen including the top layer of the police hierarchy join with underworld criminals and Mafia operators to do many things which can not be justified — rather to be abhorred. Nothing and no one can in any way tolerate such injustice in any society. The British did not teach these things to the police in the past and therefore the entire blame for such activities, if they exist, must be put on the post independence policemen/officers. An inspector general of police, it is alleged, received several thousands of gold coins and luxury gadgets for his daughter's marriage which was solemnized when he was in service. What does it mean? It means his affinity towards a section of the people who are otherwise affluent in society.As far as the duty of a police officer is concerned, every human being-the poor and the rich-is absolutely equal to all others. This equality is the basis of police-public relationship and it can only be founded on true truth and just justice in police administration. Among all the crimes which can be committed by a police officer/ man, showing insincerity to one's own uniform and disloyalty to one's oath of affirmation which every police officer/man makes at the time of his passing out from the police training institution has the characteristics making it particularly deceptive and deplorable. But, today the allegation is that in many officers'/ men's consciences, the perception towards their duties, uniform and oath of affirmation has become progressively obscured. Commission of many types of enforcement crimes by police may be a telling sign of an extremely dangerous situation. The policemen themselves need to look at the situation and find out the truth behind the allegations and call the realities by their proper names without making attempts to give justifications and explanations which may convince only them better than anybody else. There is no meaning in self-deception and if that is so, the justifications and explanations must convince others too in society. Even when a policeman wears his uniform, he may think for himself why he wears the uniform or better "Why I am a policeman?".

A retired director general of police once contacted a district superintendent of police and requested him to do some service. In reply, the director general was told "this problem, that problem and many problems". The director general of police felt sorry for having contacted a one time "subordinate"-who always said "Yes sir, No sir" to his commands. He also remembered his invitation to his house for a dinner when the assistant superintendent of police came to the State after his induction training at the National Police Academy. Whatever that be, he got in touch with a political leader and one might believe it or not, he got his services done well by the same district superintendent of police within 20-25 minutes. The director general then said: "For, if men use the green wood like this, what will happen when it is dry?" (LK.,23:31, Bible)

'Copper' is a slang in the United States and it means a 'policeman'. From this 'Copper' comes 'Cop' which means a "Policeman". I do not know why Americans call the policeman a 'cop' and when I went to the United States, some asked me: "Are you a cop?" I said : "no" and yet I do not know why the Americans use the slang 'cop' for policeman! Similar slangs are seen in other languages and people address policemen by 'slangs' in many countries all throughout the world. Why?

Policeman means a member of the police service and it includes all from constables to the director general of police in India. In current parlance, a policeman in India means a police constable and I know that it is a misnomer as the word includes all in police. It is in this sense the word is used in the title of the book. "Why I am not a Policeman?" — and it means everyone in police service and each one is expected to offer respectful service to people. The police in India have an eviable past mixed with a lot of criticisms for their human rights unfriendly attitudes and approaches. Even after India became independent, the police continued to be made the target of severe public criticism for many things they did. Police in India was late to understand that they have to divorce themselves from the past colonial culture and become truely democratic in their attitude and approaches. Of late, they have clearly understood that there could be no true democracy unless they accepted every person's dignity and showed due respect to his/her rights. Still later, they have further learnt that there could be no true peace, unless they policed the society with public's participation. Every crime-no matter it is committed by police or others — is an attack on peace and with people's participation, it can be investigated and prosecuted. It is only through people's participation, the police can maintain law and order. All these aspects are discussed in various chapters in this book. The chapters have been written during a period of five years from 1995.

I need to thank only three-my wife, Mary and our two daughters, Neethu and Neethie. They assisted me in many ways and I did not, often, say 'thank you' to them as I thought that their services were taken for granted. This is my 36th book in my area of interest, viz, crime, police and justice. They were there behind me always and everytime.

I make my views and opinions and I do so on the basis of my researches and observations on the subject. They have nothing to do with my office. It is clarified that the views and opinions expressed in this book are personal and they do not reflect the views and opinions of the Central Government, State Governments police departments and home offices. Dr. James Vadackumchery affirms that he has the moral rights to be identified as the author of this title.

I thank M/s. Kaveri Books, New Delhi for bringing out this title in print.

Crmgst. Dr. James Vadackumchery

1

Why I am not a Policeman ?

Once I was delivering a lecture at the National Institute of Criminology and Forensic Scince, Ministry of Home Affairs, Government of India, New Delhi. A participant, a deputy inspector general of police by designation, asked me: "Are you a police officer ?" I did not know what he meant by "*a police officer*". According to Indian Police Act-1861, there are a number of duties which the policeman is to perform in society. He has to protect life and property of people. I protect the life and property of many people-of myself, my dependents, my family and to some extent of my neighbours, relations, friends, kith and kin. Yes, certainly I am a policeman in that sense. Primarily, I have the responsibility to protect my person and property and so do I. Then I protect the same of others and a policeman too does the same thing–may be officially for a salary. Everybody is a policeman in the above sense. I do not think that the participant to the training programme in Delhi meant the same thing in the way I thought about a policeman.

When I was a little kid, my grandmother used to frighten me telling that she would call the policeman if I did not take food in time or eat well. Even today, I listen to my next door neighbour — mother of little Appus-doing the same thing which my grandmother did about forty nine years ago. Policeman is symbolized as a *frightener* of children and the game works well as the children eat food or obey their parents without further questioning. Was it what he meant by asking me whether or not I was a police officer? Definitely not: yet the policeman means this as well to many people. I do not think that it is the correct picture of a policeman in society, nevertheless, many still entertain this perverted view of a policeman!

I think that nobody can define a policeman nor can anybody describe him. Many people speak about policeman without knowing what they speak. The word had special meaning during the British raj, but today, the meaning is different from what it was about half a century ago. During the British rule, the policeman was a government servant and after independence, he has been a public servant. But, most dishearteningly enough many policemen — the hierarchy as a whole — did not understand the distinction between government servant and public servant so much so that the police sub-culture prevailing during the British regime continued to dominate and guide police behaviour. That is the precise reason why Appu's mother, even today, frightens her little baby by uttering the word 'policeman'.

What is a Policeman?

That is what the people do not understand even today. They have still misconceptions about the policeman and his duties. I too think that the policeman himself does not know what he is! There are many aspects for a policeman. The first is one of a legal nature — namely, that he is to execute everything legally entrusted to him. I am not interested to enumerate the duties of a policeman given in police standing orders or in other statutes. If a policeman does not perform the duties which he is legally bound to do, then I do not think that he can be honestly called a policeman. Then, further than that, most of the people also do not know what are the statutorily entrusted duties of the policeman. People see what the policeman does and makes impressions about police duties. Policeman exercises authority which he has — which he does not have — which he thinks he has and so to say, the people are at their wit's end as to what exactly are the duties of a policeman. I think that such a policeman gives wrong signals and false impressions about the policeman's duties and responsibilities. Policeman has many statutorily conferred powers and responsibilities and he must restrict his behaviour within the permitted limits. If he does not do so, he is rejected by the people and I do not want to see such a policeman in a bad shape.

The second is one of human nature — namely, the policeman must exercise his duties and powers in a human way and people friendly manner. Some people tell me that power and authority blind certain policemen and they do not know what they are doing, why they are doing and how they are doing. I saw once a superintendent of police cheerfully and with pleasure serving a suspension order to one of his teachers when he underwent police training. After serving the suspension order to his one time teacher, he said to his colleagues afterwards that he had the unique privilege of serving a suspension order to his subordinate. Heavens forgive him! He forgot to understand that the power and authority have nobler meanings in human life. I do not know how one learns such reprehensible behaviour when he wears the police uniform. I do not want to be a policeman if such behavioural patterns creep into one's personality-just like that, unconsciously. When a member of the Legislative Assembly said 30 years ago in the House that a man was different from a man in police uniform! I did not know what he really meant by that. But, now I understand the exact meaning of his utterings in the House. Any police duty-legally entrusted or otherwise performed by a policeman without a human face does not merit public appreciation. A policeman is a man first and a gentleman in every sense. Policeman is not a word, but a paragraph pregnant with human qualities and I think that he must be so.

Existence of Policeman

I do not want to write a police history-or-how organized police system came into existence in India. Let the historians do it. But, I can say that the policeman exists today. He exercises his powers — the powers conferred on him by the people. The man found out in his wisdom that he needs a police system to look after his welfare and to enable him to live in harmony with other people. Whatever might be the compelling circumstance which forced people to establish an organized police system in the country, I am not keen to enumerate them. Yet, I shall take a few of them.

Prevention of Crime

If crimes were prevented in toto, then this earthly life would be heavenly. But, crimes can not be prevented permanently, for, human nature consists of man's capacity to commit crimes as well. If violation of penal laws is a crime, surely there will be many violations. Where there is a law; there will be violations as well. Violations of law can be prevented it there is a vigil against it and so long as the vigil lasts, there may not be law violations. Policeman is expected to keep a vigil against law violations and he can not do it always on a permanent basis. Yet, he keeps a vigil and the society wants to have people to keep vigil on man's activities. Policeman is paid for the vigil he keeps on people who keep vigil on police activities?

By patrolling, surveillance, collection of intelligence, beat, cultivation of sources etc.. the policeman gets information on many things and thus he keeps a vigil on the people entrusted to his responsible care and concern. While he keeps a vigil on people and crime-doers for the sole purpose of preventing crimes, he is being watched by the people around him. The vigil thus becomes reciprocal-i.e., the police keep vigil on people and the people keep vigil on the police. Police see the crimes committed by people and they initiate action on the same. The people observe many types of enforcement crimes committed by police and they form impressions about the police and sometimes react against such police behaviours. It may be true that a policeman goes to a liquor shop to get changes for a one hundred rupee, but the policeman can not insist that the people who see the behaviour must always believe that he goes there regularly to get changes for a hundred rupee note. People have got more eyes than all the policemen can have and they may see more of police behaviour than what the police see among the people. If police service is meant to prevent crimes, then people must not see the policemen committing crimes — they be corruption, torture, partiality, political interest or whatever.

Can the people prevent crimes without the police? They thought earlier that they could not. But, now they feel they can. They take precautions and do many things at their cost to protect themselves and their property. The policemen today accept the fact that no crime can be prevented without people's wholehearted participation and support. In spite of the police, many crimes take place and the extent/intensity of invisible crimes may be very extensive and deep. There is no reason to justify why the policeman still thinks that he prevents crime and if at all he prevents the commission of crimes, what types of crimes, he is able to prevent? Does he prevent convictional crimes?-white collar crimes? enforcement crimes? communal crimes — political crimes ?-invisible crimes? Of course, he may be able to prevent some *law and order crimes* or *conventional and traditional* crimes of less serious nature. If that is so, how long can he prevent such crimes? Perhaps, I need not speak more on this point.

Investigation of Crimes

Once there was a debate, the topic being: 'is prevention of crime more important than investigation of crime?' Some participants argued that any man could prevent some crimes and the police needed only to extend their support for the people to reach the objectives. There is a point in what they said. According to them, investigation of crime was something which the police alone could do under the law. Hence they concluded that the existence and survival of police were justified more on the basis of their responsibility to investigate crimes than to prevent the same. Arguments have counter arguments and people investigated crimes and awarded punishments even at a time organized police system was not in existence. Even today, some people do the same and are not even prepared to report to police about all crimes that take place amidst them. After investigation, they award punishments including victim compensation. Forget about the penal laws. People violate social laws, cultural laws, religious laws, ethical laws, institutional laws etc... and such violations are not investigated by the police. Yet, justice is administered. Every society — be it a tribal society or an advanced society — develops its system of justice administration and organized police is a system thus created and developed by the society. People thought that it was better to have such a specialized group for investigation of crime and thus the police system came into being. It was thought to be a convenient system provided the investigation of crime was conducted in a just, fair and human rights friendly manner. History has ample evidence to show that investigation of crime contained a lot of informal arrests, illegal detention, concoction of evidence, manipulation of records, production of tutored and false witnesses etc.. The laws were enacted from time to time to remedy the maladies, yet one could notice violations of these laws in many ways and the violators were the enforcement agencies themselves. Enforcement crimes thus received a distinct identity and I have discussed them in detail in my book '*Police, Enforcement Crimes and (In) Justice*'. I do not propose to elaborate on the same because that again would take a lot of space in this book. Nobody, even the enforcement agencies, does not want to commit enforcement crimes to prove a crime against a guilty accused. Policemen now find that a great many things they did in the past were not necessary if they were prepared to have recourse to scientific and psychological ways of investigating crimes. But, they do not possess adequate information and technical knowhow to investigate crimes in scientific way.

I do not know how was the conviction rate in the cases tried by courts after police investigation during the British past. But, now I know that the conviction rate is going down in an alarmingly shocking way. The reasons may be many and one can enumerate the inadequacy of laws, proaccused attitude of courts, lack of cooperation from the people, unethical strategies adopted by defence lawyers as the possible causes of large scale acquittals. All these explanations and justifications can not help to build up public trust and confidence on police investigation. When more and more criminal cases are acquitted by courts, it shakes the very foundation of people's initial plans to set up an organization-a police system — to investigate crimes. The people ask: "why should we invest so much money and manpower to get a low turn out from the investigation of crimes?". If the police argue that crimes are investigated just to give victim satisfaction and to offer assurance to people that no criminal will be allowed to commit crimes without undergoing the punishment prescribed for his act, then they have an obligation to convince the people that criminals are convicted. As more and more crimes are acquitted, the police become less respectable before the people. 'Why I am a policeman?' — the question can be answered only if he is able to convince the people that he is doing the job in a manner expected of him — to the full satisfaction and expectations of the people who are the patrons and sponsors of the policeman.

Law and Order Maintenance

Police Acts emphatically say that law and order maintenance is a police duty and the people justify the existence and survival of police on the ground that there must be a lawfully authorized agency to maintain law and order in a society. No doubt, even before organized policing came into existence, law and order was maintained in the society then existed.

Many people who live in society are not threats to the law and order. It is a minority of people who cause problems for law and order and the success of police work depends upon how well they identify the people, sources and forces which create law and order problems. A drunkard on a road, an affray at a junction, a street gathering, a procession on a road, road blocks, strikes and demonstrations etc.. may be creating law and order problems and the police is an effective machinery to deal with such situations. Police officers who are trained well can manage any law and order situation with restraint and tact. In a democracy, law and order situations may emerge at any time and a well disciplined police service can tackle it effectively, sometimes using minimum force. There must be good planning and effective operation well designed in advance.

After a law and order management, the people must feel that it was managed *well* by the police. Law and order problems are managed so that the people live again in harmony. But, sometimes, the management takes a rather curious form. For instance, it is argued that rifles, lathies and tear gas shells are given to police for managing law and order situations. But, they must be used only in absolutely necessary situations. For, the policeman is accountable for everything he does during a law and order situation. Commissions of Inquiry are appointed to see whether or not the police use their lathies, rifles and teargas shells in the right way. The rifles are designed in such a way that when it is triggered, the bullet hits on the target and in a law and order situation, it may be a human target. All the powers and the authority the police have should be used with prudence and wisdom. If someone says that the police have the powers and authoirty for them to use in the way they want them to be used, it is nonsense. They do not have unlimited powers and authority. I think that the authority and the power which the police have are intended not to make human life miserable, rather to make it happier. This must be the guiding principle. A policeman who is not able to understand this truth will prove himself to be a failure.

"Why I am not a Policeman?"-I am not a policeman because I do not have the required aptitude to become a law and order manager. Once a police officer said: "I am a good investigator of crime and I want to be an investigator. But, I am not understood properly by my superiors. I am always told to manage law and order situations". In police, a proper assessment of one's aptitude and interest is seldom done meaningfully so much so that many who are unfit to hold certain positions are forced to do certain things which they do not like. Miserable indeed!

Traffic Control

Orginally, people did not think of entrusting the traffic control duty for the police.The reasons were that then there were no vehicles for the police to control. I think that the duty was later added to police functions. I used to think: "why should the police control traffic?". In all States, Motor Vehicle Departments function and can they not do the job? I can understand that the police must be entursted with the duty of investigating traffic accidents, for, it consists of professional police work. In traffic control, what is the role of police?

In many minor Acts, police have concurent jurisdiction with other law enforcement agencies. Why should the police be dragged into areas where other functionaries work/should work. Why to milk-feed other man's baby? This creates murmur in many. The entire traffic control must be entrusted to the motor vehicles departments. If the motor vehicles departments need more personnel, it must be done. Transport and communication are fast developing and therefore just like the telecommunication department, the motor vehicles department must be enlarged. The police department must not be overburdened with traffic control duties. Most of the traffic offences are not criminal offences committed with a *mens rea* and therefore police investigation is not warranted. Today, students, N.S.S volunteers and many others come forward to help the authorities to effect traffic control. It must be encouraged and the police duties must be limited only to traffic accident cases in which police investigation becomes necessary. Today, police and road users do not have desirable human relations so much so that many complaints are received against the police. Traffic enforcement officers have an instructional role more than investigating crimes. It being so, the duties must be entrusted entirely to the motor vehicle department. The laws must be amended to this effect if that is necessary. The formation which the police get today may not be conducive to perform an instructional role on roads. The rifles, lathies, tear-gas shells,. criminal procedure code, forensic experts, lie-detection machines, unarmed combat, interrogation, arrests, bail etc. are not required for performing the instructional role on roads. The police ego is not what is required for a traffic law enforcement officer. "I need not be a policeman to do the job of a traffic law enforcement officer" — say many policemen.

Justice Administration

People think that policemen must be there to administer justice to people. No doubt, there is great injustice in the world and often the good suffers, and often the wicked prospers in this world. Domestic injustice, consumer-injustice, caste injustice, communal injustice, labour-injustice, injustice to unborn children, injustice to the old and infirm, injustice to children, injustice to the poor, to the oppressed, to the weak, to the handicapped, to the helpless and thus one can see a variety of jnjustices in the world. What can or what should the police do to fight against all these may be seen? The police are not expected, meant or paid for fighting all such injustices.

Criminal justice had been in existence ever since man came into the world. Some sort of policing and punishing the crime-doers were too there ever since. Organized policing came into the world for administering or aiding the administration of criminal justice. Now the police are expected to administer criminal justice, victim justice, gender justice, human rights justice, juvenile justice, just justice under an equal justice system which I have dealt with in detail. in my book *Indian Police and Equal Justice Under Law.* The police are not able to ensure all these '*justices*' to people owing to several barriers.

"Why I am not a policeman?"-some good meaning police officers say that they can not administer justice of any kind to people as they are handcuffed. Political pressures, pressures from the department, pressures from the social higher ups, pressures from the affluent, the corrupt and unjust people incapaciate them to administer justice to people. Police officers/men who do not yield to powerful pressures are subjected to many road-blocks in their works. The push and pull factors operate so powerfully in such a way that the policemen helplessly yield to such pressures. People who speak of fair justice administration come forward in large numbers to defeat the ends of justice.

Emotional Aspects of Police Justice

People and the police think that there is something called '*Police justice*'and what they mean by it, I think, is a sort of infliction of pain-social, physical and psychological-to crime-doers in a police way. What is the police way? People tell me that the police way of justice means to them harassment, social humiliation or employment of torture. Handcuffing a person just to humiliate him, shouting at people by epithets, manhandling the suspect to elicit confessions etc.. are brought as examples for administering police justice. Human rights activists object to any sort of police justice as they think that it is not the justice envisaged by the Constitution and civilized people in the international community.

I think that there is an emotional content in some of police actions. Policemen evaluate a crime from many angles and they see the victims in front of them. They identify themselves with the victims of crime and sometimes behave on behalf of the victims. In such situations, emotions play a great role. I have asked some policemen: "Why do you become emotional when you deal with crime-doers?". They say: "owing to an excess of laws in favour of the suspects in crime, the crime-doers think that the investigating officers are helpless in front of them. There are many people-including lawyers and human rights activists — who come forward to help the suspects/crime-doers and no such people come for the victims of the offence. This makes us to become emotional". A superintendent of police once asked me: "A suspect who has hidden the stolen property once told me that he had nothing to tell ,me about the place where he had hidden the stolen property. His lawyers said that he had a right to keep silence and then how to break his silence". I know that the situation causes tension in police interrogator and he may lose control over himself. He may become emotional or better, any person in his position becomes emotional. A police interrogator is not a superhuman being and no one can become superhuman on this earthly world although some may wish to be so. The press, people, criminals, courts, lawyers and even gods become emotional at times and a policeman is not an exception.

"Why I am not a policeman?" — I am not because, I can not be a superhuman individual. Everyone wants the policeman to be superhuman when he interacts with people who sometimes become subhuman or worse than human beings. People do not understand that superhuman beings are not intended to interact with human and sub-human beings. In communal violence, political crimes, strikes and agitations, people practice every kind of cruelty and the policeman can not keep his eyes shut to such realities. Peace and harmony are established not always by supernatural behaviour-not by intelligence alone, but by strategies which are charged by emotions as well. There is an argument that the policeman may become emotional, but should not go to the extent of becoming irrational. Often, the irrationality of the policeman is attacked by people as they say "the more one becomes irrational, the more he becomes cruel in his approaches".

People accept the police, not because they do not want to reject their services but because that is the only system now available for them to police the society. Many tribal communities police the tribal groups not by organized police service, but by themselves. Even in the past, when organised police service was not available, people did police their societies. Hence, to think that a society can not survive without an organised police service is not right. For, every society will develop its own police service in someway or other. Whenever an organised police system does not satisfy the people in the way it must, then the society may devise its own methods to protect it. Private security services and private detective agencies are in operation now. Some private financiers have their "men" for enforcing their laws and they are doing many things which the police were doing once upon a time. If police use third degree methods or employ torture on suspects, people bring human rights activists and lawyers to protect them. If the organised police service does somethings against people's expectations, the press brings them out. In cultural programmes the police are rediculed. There is an allegation against police that the organized police system has been reponsible for miscarriage of justice in society. One may find any number of accusations against the police-be they corruption, concoction, manipulation or mismanagement — and the police as an organized group could prove that the system was free from allegations.

How do the Police Regard Their Own Activities?

I think that many police officers/men believe that they do the right things always. A certain number of people who are acquitted by courts of law are found to be totally innocent ones! Likewise, a certain number of people convicted-stuides show-are also innocent ones! Take another case. In the ISRO spy case, ultimately it was proved (court too accepted it) that the suspects were innocent. But, if everything the suspects in the case told was true, then it was surely a cruel episode. This is, as said earlier, just an example. There are a great many ways in which, at the present moment, the police by its various methods of administering justice, inflicts upon people unserved and unnecessary sufferings. The police have developed certain methods and strategies of questionable nature and which have nothing much to do with human happiness and administration of justice.

What has human happiness to do with administration of justice? What has human happiness to do with police administration of justice? The object of police interrogation, investigation of crime, torture of suspects, concoction of evidence etc.. may not be to make the people happy. They may be to prove a crime against the suspects or for the ego-happiness. Such behaviours and strategies could create a sort of fear of police among the people. People look at the police in fear — in trembling when in uniform and look at them with indifference and contempt when not in service. Retired police officers/men may attest the arguments in a strong way. Police, during the British period, I think, survived by causing terror and fear among the people (cf. Torture Commission Report). The fear and terror continued to dominate police sub-culture even after India became independent in 1947. And still, the fear and terror are seen in a lesser intensity and degree in many police interactions with people or that is what studies conducted in this area reveal and what people speak about its show.

People honestly tell that they are not able to predict the police behaviour when they interact with the police. Sunddenly and surprisingly, some police interrogators become hot tempered and aggressive. Fear forms the basis of police-public interactions i.e., the fear of torture, the fear of indecent behaviour, the fear of humiliation, the fear of harassment, the fear of being called epithets etc... Fear, I think, keeps the people away from police and the awareness of police that the people have fear and terror of them make them to behave in a cruel and aggressive way. Hence, there is no wonder that cruelty and policing have gone hand in hand.

The fear which the people have towards the police must be eradicated if they must come closer to police. Any attempt to reorient the attitude of police may not yield results unless the fear of the people is eliminated. Once I was attending a seminar organized by the High Court Bar Association. A retired judge presented a paper and he said: "I, honestly speaking, do fear the police". He was a retired judge and if he felt so, how would an ordinary man fear the police? At another time, an inspector general of police said in another seminar that he too feared the policeman. Even after 23 years of my service at the police training college as a teacher, I too am fearful of the police and mostly they are my students. No, I do not want to be a policeman, for, I don't want to identify myself as a "FEAR" in society!

Some police officers still believe that our society can be policed only by causing fear and terror among the people. Of course, it may work to some extent to police the society. I think that fear and terror will not and can not bring police and the people closer. Perhaps, it is one of the main reasons why people still maintain an avoiding attitude to police. How far can the causing of fear among the people help to control crimes? As the police is not the principal agency that controls crime in any society (this aspect is dealt with in detail in the next chapter), deterrence and causing of fear among people may have only limited effect upon the commission of crimes by people. People do commit crimes-not in police visibility, but away from police and often under precautions taken for not detecting crimes.

The police must look at the people not as criminals always. People are good, bad, beautiful, ugly, law abiding, law violating and precisely therefore look at them as they are. Never think that terror, deterrence or causing of fear can help the people to be law abiding. Try to be close with the people by being one among them and not by frightening them. The police have inherited many misconceptions from the British police, but is it not high time that the Indian police divorce themselves from their ugly past? Police have to have self-esteem and must look at the people giving due respect to their human dignity. A good police need an upright conscience, courage and a human face. There is no meaning in looking back to the British past, for, past is dead and gone.

Police and Justice

Many police officers say that justice can never be administered without the police. I do not know what do they mean by '*justice*'. For them, justice may be a subjective concept and for others, it may be more objective than subjective. As to justice, a great deal depends upon how one understands that concept. Employment of torture on a suspect may be *justice* for a police interrogator, but is not so for the suspect and human rights activists. Once a police officer became paralysed and people around him said that he deserved such a poetic justice. Why did they say so? They argued that he had tortured many innocent people while he was in service and God waited till he retired to award the punishment — i.e., paralysis. I do not know how far can we accept the peoeple's arguments on the paralysis. But, they thought honestly that it was "justice" to the police officer. A primary school teacher became paralysed and the same people did not say that he was administered poetic justice for the ill-doings he committed. Why? They had sympathy for the primary school teacher while they had vengeance to the police officer. Both had the same misery and agony, but the people looked at them from different angles. In one case, the paralysis and consequent sufferings were justified whereas they were not justified in the other case. This may show that what the people want is not police justice — whatever may be the concepts the policemen give to it — but just justice as expected by the people and the society. Realizing this, some police officers/men want to work in special units where they do not have to enforce *police justice* instead of *just justice* under law. I saw once a christian police officer keeping a crucifix on his table. I asked him: "Why do you keep this crucifix?". He told me then: "I look at the crucifix before I take a decision. It gives me tremendous satisfaction as I can not but do justice as the Lord desires it to be administered by me". It means that there is "justice" which is different from *Police justice* as conceived and enforced by some in police service. "I am a policeman, for, I want to administer justice as I am authorized by law and people to do so" — this must be the approach of a real policeman who thinks that his authority to administer justice is a gift given to him from above-not out of his merit, but out of the grace of the Almighty.

I have as well seen some Hindu officers keeping photographs of certain holy swamijies and gods on their tables. They pray to them so that they get the right sense to administer justice. Some have finger rings having the pictures of gods/swamijies and they too have a lot of faith on their blessings. "Right justice, through right paths and means" — that is what they want from their gods and holy swamijies. They say that the justice must be objective and that must not be the 'police justice' in the conventional sense of the terms.

Superstition plays, sometimes, a role in administration of justice. There are constables as well as directors general of police who believe in occult practices and evil spirits. There is a belief in some parts of India and it says that people who are seated in office facing north kill their enemies — and those who face west live happily in service. I do not know how far is the belief true and objective. But I have seen a good number of officers seated facing west than north. I have also seen that officers who face north believe in occult practices and invoke evil spirits to destroy their enemies. I do not know how far or how much their beliefs and superstitions affect their sense of justice. At the same time, I have noticed that God fearing police officers and those who respect human values administering just justice more honestly than those who believe in occult practices, evil spirits and demenological influences. However I have seen hypocritcs even among the holy believers in God and values. They deceive God, men and themselves and administer justice. Certainly, they damage the reputation of the department and the meaning of justice administration.

A superintendent of police once told: "The director general of police is an upright man although he is a womanizer". I do not understand how does the uprightness of the director general of police go with his womanizing nature! Certainly, such a director general will fail to administer just justice to people — whatever may be his position and sense of justice. Logically it follows that any corrupt — human rights unfriendly — vulnerable to influences- police officer/man will not be able to administer just justice. Many police officers/men are not free from allegations of something or another and precisely therefore many people entertain a view whether or not they will administer justice. People lose their trust and confidence on police sense of justice.

Police and Dharma

I have very little knowledge about Dharma, but I know that Dharma refers to that which is right. I used to tell my trainees in the police college that any police officer/man who administers justice in accordance to law and procedure established by law in a lawful manner, then he is doing *Dharma*. Police-each individual in police service by virtue of its character occupies a special position in society. Each policeman/officer has his proper responsibilities and he has to perform his duties in a responsible manner. He has to be guided by objective norms of behaviour accepted by the people in a democracy and the law of the land. He must not be guided by his own instincts, urges, passions, emotions and interests. The allegation is that the power blinds many in police service and resultantly they forget about their *Dharma* to people and society. Resultantly, many police officers/men do not receive due recognition which they ought to receive.

When I gave a lecture to the jail officers, one of them told me: "Sir, many *rapists* who are convicted and are coming to prisons are not real rapists".

I then asked: "what do you mean?"

He said: "They are victims of police action on false complaints by those who have sex relations by mutual consent".

I said: "You mean rape by victim participation?". He said: "Yes, there you are Sir".

If his version is true, I may say that the investigating officers fail in their *Dharma* to administer just justice.

Once I saw an inspector general of police (vigilance) weaping and I saw some files in front of him. I asked him: "Why do you weep?".

He said: "I have two sets of files. One related a fraud committed by a public servant and the amount involved was 98 lakhs. The other related to a class IV employee who accepted a bribe and the amount involved was Rs. 50. I have no clear and sufficient legal evidence to prosecute the former while I have more than enough legal evidence to prosecute the latter. What to do and how to go about? What is my Dharma here?

Dharma means righteousness and it sustains the individual, human society and the world. Police community too comes within the purview of the operation of Dharma . I made inquiries about that inspector general of police and I could know that he was a man of upright conscience. Many people tell me that it is these sorts of men who maintain the dignity of the police department and the public trust on police system. Police department without a *dharma*-consciousness will be hollow and a director general of police, as pointed out, with womanizing tendencies is a dishonour to the department. I know an additional director general of police who speaks always dharma, but he drinks foreign liquor and smokes costly foreign cigerettes. He has an immoral past too. I then used to think that "if a poor man eats chicken, either the chicken is sick or the poor man is sick". There is no third option. Likewise, the people thought about the above director general as a person who utters empty words.

Justice administration without dharma consciousness is hollow and that is the reason why police ethics is taught to new entrants to police department. A police officer/man can not be a moral "wreck". Every one has a conscience which is *"norma normata"* and not *"norma normans"* . Policeman is not an exception to this and one should not opt for police job if he does not possess a conscience which is *"norma normata"*.

Policing the Society and Responsible Policing

Both are two concepts. Policing a society by applying jungle laws is disfavoured by people and democracy. Responsible policing must always be responsible . Responsible policing has respect for law and authoirty. Do the police enforce law showing due respect to law? This is a topic which I think has not been quite sufficiently dealt with by police officers although the people in a democracy speak about it. After a lathy charge or firing this topic is discussed by people and politicians. Sometimes, commissions of inquiry are appointed to examine the issue and the police are made accountable for what they do in society. The commissions so appointed probe into for finding out whether or not there is responsible policing. Courts of law scrutinize the investigation and decides whether or not there is responsible investigation. Superiors in police watch their subordinates and see that they perform their duties in a responsible manner. The press and media too keep a watch on responsible policing. People in a democracy want the police to be responsibly responsible in their works. The concept of policing-as it was in India from the British — was mixed up with a notion that the police was a 'Force' and not a 'Service'. Many police functionaries in the past believed that the police, as a force, could employ their muscle power in the way they wanted. No one questioned their notion and insisted for responsible policing. As the police was identified as a force, people feared them. They kept the police away and wanted to keep themselves away from police. People thought that political power was necessary to overpower the police power and thus politicians started coming to police in larger numbers. Could the political power make responsible policing? No. They tried to make the police to be a force to execute their will through their muscles. The result has been that responsible policing remained as something which the people must insist for. Today, the people demand for responsible policing with due accountability and transparency.

Police — Human Relations

This is a topic I have dealt with extensively in my earlier books. I still believe that inadequate police–human relation is at least in part the cause of many problems and difficulties between the police and the people. If the police are able to understand people and the people are able to understand the police, many problems may be solved. The police depend upon the people and the people depend upon the police — this mutual dependence must be accepted in reality. I even think that some police functions can be effectively performed by people. I think that this applies especially to prevention of crimes and maintenance of law and order. People's capacity in prevention of crime and maintenance of law and order are even today underestimated by almost all police functionaries. To my mind, policing the society through people's participation has got the greatest social importance and far more likely to benefit the people and the police than the policing the society by organized policed work.

How does people's participation help policing the society? For example, let us take theft in society. If many thefts take place in an area, everybody in that area becomes disturbed. Police conduct patrolling or establish an aid post. How long can they do it?-consistently?-permanently? The moment police patrolling is stopped or the police picket is removed, thefts may be again committed. In the absence of public's participation in crime prevention, police will be able to do only very little or nothing. With public's participation, the police will be able to do wonders. If a theft takes place, the police may take many people into custody and some of them may be innocent. Interrogating a person by police as a suspect is resented against by people especially when the interrogated is found to be innocent. Police-community relations suffer as a consequence. People must be taught as to how to guard their property against thefts-how to keep vigil against thieves-how to cooperate with police in the prevention efforts etc.. Police is just a social institution and is necessary to enforce law/prevent crimes with people's participation. For this, police-human relations become inevitable. If the people can be persuaded that they themselves in the locality will be able to catch the thief-even when the police fail-it would be more effective than the police alone taking the responsibility of preventing thefts in the area. The thieves are not always caught by the police; but the public vigil itself will work as sufficeint deterrence to prevent crimes. People today inform the police when thefts take place and they do not do much to prevent thefts. This is a public strategy which must be discouraged.

In law and order matters too, the people can do wonders with the support of police. When demonstrations are held, some police officers get in touch with the leaders and work out strategies to conduct peaceful demonstrations without causing damage to public and their property. Instances are plenty to show that efficient police officers manage law and order situations efficiently by the cooperation and willing support of the people. This is demonstrated in communal tensions, in student unrests, labour disputes and political agitations.

There is a misconception in police. Some police officers still entertain the notion that police-community relations may be enhanced by participating in sports and athlectics by police, in conducting boy's clubs or in celebrating crime prevention weeks etc...almost in a ritualistic fashion for the purpose of propaganda. I do not deny the impact of such hierarchy sponsored programmes, but I think that police-community relations can be improved by ensuring public's participation in police work, particularly in crime prevention, law and order or investigation of crime. As it is, no investigation can be successfully completed without public co-operation and participation.

What is the number of policemen in a society? They are very few compared to the population and to think that these small number of policemen will be able to effect an effective control over the entire population may be wrong and is far away from being real. *Community Policing* is a new idea which is being experimentally implemented in some cities and I am told that it works well — better than the traditional policing. People see more reasons to think that policing by public participation is certainly better than the present system of policing which has outlived its utility. As it is today, even civic minded people hardly go to police to extend their help in policing the society. Why? I think that the police today do not welcome such helps as they discourage them by their negative reaction to such supports. Because of this, some people are inclined to think that the police are neither so welcoming nor so desiring of public help and support. Hence, they keep away from police,: "I am a policeman, for I am close to people-live with them — work with their support and cooperation" — this thought must come to all who wear police kakhi uniform if they want the people to come closer to them.

Police may realize the fact that people in general do not want anyone to steal their property, if at all there is no law in the Indian Penal Code defining what is theft. It is to the interest of the society that they protect their property. In such a situation, there is only added advantage that the police enlist public cooperation against thefts. Why should the police consider that it is there baby to protect the property of people? This thinking of police made them to use fair and foul means to ensure protection to people and the people find it difficult to accept all means the police adopt for the purpose. The closer the police work with the people, the better it is to maintain good human relations.

Because of the wrong approach the police maintained till now in preventing crimes, detecting criminals, investigating offences, managing law and order situations without public cooperation and support, I find among many people at the present day an indifference to police activities and strategies which I can not but think extremely non-utilitarian. When people keep away from police, for example, in extending whole-hearted support, the police find it extremely difficult to prove a crime before a court of law. Police in earlier days thought that they could ensure public support by threat and causing fear in them. But, today, I do not think that such an attitude is going to yield good results. Resultantly, criminal cases are acquitted in large numbers and people lose their confidence and trust on police. Police are accused of promoting miscarriage of justice. If public trust is lost, the reasons must be identified, and remedial measures taken. For this, the only way open to police is to establish good relations with the people. With ego projections and pasted status consciousness, no one must think that he can come closer to the people. The director general of police must get out of his car having three stars and a flag and go to the people to see that they come closer to him. Positions of authority must be open to the common man on the street. I can respect the director general of police who encourages his officers/men to go to the people rather than waiting for the people to come to them for service. There must be transparency in police work. Human rights activists may go to the extent of accusing that the police have institutionalized torture in police stations and this allegation can be wipped of only if the police become transparent to the people. If the police are not now as bad as they were in the past, that was due to the influence of those who criticized the police and due to the desire of police functionaries themselves to be transparent in their activities.

Why I am Not a Policeman?

I repeat this question in this book as I think that this is a question which every policeman must ask to himself when he enters into the third millennium. We have an organized police system established by the British in the long past and their intentions were different. No policeman could ask the question: "Why I am not a Policeman? in the British regime. They instead asked the question: "Why I am a Policeman?". He answered the question and that was how we could get a police system with the philosophy, attitude, approaches etc which we could see today in India. The Indian Police Commission: 1902-03 made further modifications in the already established police system in India. The National Police Commission: 1977-1981 made many recommendations which were not implemented till date. Now, there is no meaning in implementing any recommendations of the forsaken National Police Commission at this belated time. As it is, no one sees any movement for instituting a second National Police Commission to lead the police to the third millennium. In this desperate situation,each policeman must ask two questions to himself: (1) "Why I am a policeman?"and (2) "Why I am not a policeman?". The chapters that follow will throw light for the policemen to think about the questions in an objective way and find answers to them.

2

Police and Control of Crimes: Can They?

My own view on control of crimes (which I may commit in life) by me is that of a sceptic. For, I do not know when or whether I will commit crimes. Looking back, certainly I have violated many laws including penal laws. Many a time I was not caught or if at all I was caught, then I have escaped from punishments. My father, mother and teachers have punished me for misbehaviour and every misbehaviour is a violation of law. Who could or who can control me from committing crimes? I do not commit crimes, for, I do not want to commit crimes.

People thought that deterrence could control crimes — or causing deterrence by way of punishment could control crimes. They believed in retributive theory of criminal justice. Did the theory succeed in controlling crimes? No. History proved that crimes were on the increase in spite of retributive approaches. I am not talking about terrorists and convictional criminals. Of course, any amount of deterrence or retribution may control terrorism if the terrorists do not want to indulge in terrorists' activities. Police kill the terrorists and the terrorists kill the police in encounters. I am not talking about enforcement criminals who commit crimes while they are on duty. People involved in the control of crimes commit enforcement crimes and how can they claim that they can control crimes? History proved that there were many prison riots and people convicted several times became recidivists in spite of their incarceration. Forget about them. Retribution and deterrent approaches may not control even ordinary criminals and that is what the increase of crimes every year indicates. If that is the truth then can we say that control of crime by police is a myth? — just a myth? a wishful thinking?

Some policemen claim that they control crimes while some others do not say so. There is no consensus among the policemen themselves. If police can control illicit production and sale of liquor, then many liquor tragedies can be prevented. But, liquor tragedies are a recurring reality in the country. If Immoral Traffic (Prevention) Act and the powers vested on police by the Act can stop prostitution, then there may not be prostitutes anywhere in the country. If section 302 IPC can deter murderers and potential murderers, then there may not be murder in the subcontinent. Some people from Andaman and Nicobar islands say that transportation was once upon a time a deterrent punishment and the forefathers of some of them were deterrently transported to the Island. They call their crimes "*blessed crimes*", for they are what they are today because of the punishment awarded to their forefathers.

On analysis of the penal history, one may notice that crimes are recurring in society and precisely therefore the police claim that they are in society to control crimes. I have interviewed some recidivists in crimes and they emphatically said that the police could not control their activities. Some of the recidivists are criminologists in a real sense and therefore they put forward a theory which is: "existence of police does not help to control crimes. Rather, the criminals and potential criminals take adequate precautions when they commit crimes so that they are not caught by the police". I do not want to comment on their theory, yet I may propose that every society has a quantum of crime and the people, somehow or other, commit crimes so that the crimes in a society do not go beyond a certain level. Hence, control of crime by police in any case does not guarantee the birth and existence of a crimeless society. The legend of Mahabali says that there was a crimeless society and the king Mahabali was pushed down to "Pathalam" which was a place from where he could not rule.

How can a crimeless society be created when the reality is such that crimeless society does not and can not exist. If crimes can not be annihilated, then they must be controlled. For this purpose, police was created. The truth is that crimes exist in spite of police and they show an increasing trend as days go on. Then the question: "Why should there be police?". The question can be answered if one tries to find out an answer to the question: "What type of crimes do the police control?". In the previous chapter, a casual mention about the type of crimes the police prevent has been made. Ordinary men are affected by ordinary type of crimes. Patrolling by police can control and prevent crimes when the police are on patrol duty. The criminals may commit the crime when the patrolling is over. Likewise, the presence of the police at a particular spot may prevent the crime-doers from committing crimes so long as the police presence is ensured at that particular spot. Surveillance by police may prevent crimes in so far as the criminals are under surveillance. Beat may prevent crimes so long as the beat constable is active. The question is: "What type of crime do they prevent?" Can the police conduct patrolling for 24 hours a day, seven days a week? twelve months a year? Can the police conduct beat everywhere in the jurisdiction — always? No. They can not. The constant patrolling, beat, surveillance etc.can create an awareness among the people of the police vigil and the unnoticed or invisible police vigil has only limited effectiveness in controlling ordinary crimes. More serious crimes like murder, kidnapping, rape, burglary may take place even when the awareness of police persists in society. Of course, they may not take place in the presence of police. For, the presence of police is one thing and the awareness of police vigil with little visibility of the same is another thing. *Goondas*, underworld criminals, organized rackeetering, Mafia operations etc., are seen even when an awareness of police vigil with little visibility exists in a particular locality.

When the police keep a constant vigil in a particular area, the crimes that take place in that area go to another place where the police vigil is minimum or non-existent. Raids for the manufacture and sale of illicit liquor has been organized in a particular locality. It was later found that the same was reduced there, but was more profitably started in another area including transportation of illicit liquor from other States where the criminals could conduct their operations with freedom.

The word "crime" is used nowadays in a very loose sense. Acts/omissions against the penal laws are strictly called offences under law. There are many "crimes" which are not "offences" under law. Commission agents, corruption agents, Mafia criminals, organised racketeers, investment frauds, advertisement frauds, goondaism, authority sponsored crimes, enforcement crimes etc.. are crimes, but they are said to be crimes in a loose way. But, murder, rape, forgery, kidnappings etc.. which are defined in the Indian Penal Code as early as 1860 are called crimes-heneous crimes for which penalties are prescribed. A conscientious policeman may say that various investment frauds which are not strictly defined as *crimes* in the Penal Code can be interpretted as a "Fraud" just like any other frauds committed under the Penal laws. A petty fraud may be treated as seriously as an investment fraud which causes irrepairable damages and financial loss to the people. The section on *'cheating'* defined in the Penal Code in 1860 was not drafted with an intention to deal with the present day investment frauds. Many crimes which are seen today were not even known to those who drafted the Indian Penal Code in 1860. As such the policeman is helplessly seeing the various crimes currently committed by "sharks" in society while he concentrates only on the traditional types of crimes which are seen among all people in society. Crimes are human acts and very much a social fact —

this loose perception which the criminologists had about a century ago is not valid now as many crimes are *calculated* human act for which the etiological explanations given by criminologists earlier can no longer apply. The definition given to crimes in 1860 have very little to do with the crimes which the 'sharks' in society commit today. Many of the crimes which the "sharks" commit can not be proceeded against as they hold the key to the framing of law and justice administration. Like any other privileged community, they use their power for their advantage. The legislators, businessmen, bureaucrats, enforcement officers have a nexus which make them to indulge in organized racketeering, Mafia operations, and underworld criminal activities. The policeman with a Penal Code in his hand looks at such privileged people in helplessness. The privileged people indulge in the commission of crimes to make profits and the crimes they commit are business and money for them. Any policeman who raises his hand against them will be crushed to nothingness. In effect, there is nobody to compel them from committing crimes. As they can not be forced by any authority to desist from their wicked acts, they continue to flourish in society. What happened to the Ministers in Government who indulged in crimes involving multi-crores? — to the share brokers, bulls and bears? - to the bureaucrats who received kickbacks? — to the commission agents who made fortunes in life? Many top level investigators who seriously investigated the crimes under the existing penal laws were transferred out — were forced to resign from services — were evicted from the office — were retired on superannuation and the investigation progresses at a slow pace. The policeman with his traditional knowledge about preventive strategies of crime continues to conduct patrolling, beat, surveillance etc... thinking that he controls crimes in society.

Police and their Attitude Towards Crimes

The worst feature of the police in India, however, is said to be its attitude towards crimes — an attitude so morbid and so unnatural that they consider IPC crimes as the only crimes to be prevented. They know that many penal sections in the Indian Penal Code have outlived their utility and are of no use now. Yet, they think that they are the crimes which must be prevented for social progress and prosperity. We sometimes hear talks to the effect that the police succeeded in controlling and preventing crimes. It is necessary to say so repeatedly so that the government in power may claim that it is doing something wonderful. We may say that political crimes and murders have been prevented by the present government in power. What do we mean by that? People who do not know the exact definition of *political murder* or the concept of *political crimes* make such statements! They have an impression that crimes committed by politicians are political crimes. If a murder has been committed by a politician, they say that it is a political murder. Political murders are not politicians committing murders. Any politician who commits a murder is not a political murderer. Without understanding the meaning and concept of political crimes, they make announcements and thereby some of them politicize crimes. I have discussed in my book '*Crime and Society: Current Issues and Trends*' about politicisation of criminals and criminalization of politics. Both are crimes in the real sense and the police as an agency can not prevent such crimes. A crime is a crime, no matter who commits it and if that is accepted, then there is no sense in politicising a crime which politicians have done. Politicians, when they commit crimes-traditional or current—may be able to manage and manipulate matters to their favour. Politicians are found involved in sex-rackets, sweet heart contracts with business magnets, amassing wealth beyond the known sources of income and what not? How can the police prevent their crimes? This is an area which has not attained sufficient criminological attention today.

Concepts of crime which are bound up with the traditional notions and definitions seen in the Penal Code are ones which do an extraordinary amount of harm to prevention and investigation of current models of crime by the police. The traditional notions of crime which the police have today afford the people an outlet for their vested interests which they believe can be encashed for their advantage by involving in committing new forms of crimes. Take, for example, a person conducts ISD telephone frauds which may be as follows. A person in India, suppose, has two telephones with ISD facilities. A person who wants to make a telephone call to Singapore from U.S.A. makes a call to India and request the Indian telephone holder to connect him to a number in Singapore. In other words, the American books a telephone call to Singapore via the telephone holder in India. The Indian telephone holder calls the Singapore number and also he calls the U.S.A. number and allows the American to talk to Singapore via his minitelephone exchange in India. The charge for the Singapore call is collected in U.S.A. at a rate higher than what is existing in India and lower than what is existing in U.S.A. The racket thus makes enormous amount of money by this method. Strictly speaking, the Indian here does not violate any law which exists in India, for, he pays the telephone bill as per Indian rates. But, the American cheats the U.S. Telephone Establishment and the question is: "What can be done to book the racketeers? In order to prevent these sorts of frauds, it is necessary to make laws defining the offences, but so long as no law is in force, the racketeers make money by their nefarious activities. I can not understand how well can the police control such crimes as long as they do not have any control over the telecom services in the Country?

It is not only in regard to the notions of crime but also in regard to the lack of knowledge in the prevention and control of the present day crimes that the police are not able to do what they ought to. Police are inclined to think that the new crimes do not come in the purview of police's preventive functions. For example, income tax frauds and tax - evations, the police think, do not come within the preventive strategies of police. On the contrary, a simple theft and a small scale burglary, they think, come within their power to control and prevent. They may initiate steps to prevent such thefts/burglaries.They may not have any interest to prevent income-tax or insurance frauds. It is estimated that several crores of rupees are lost by way of bank frauds, but the police are not keen about them although they may be interested to stop affrays or simple hurts by people. The police may investigate such frauds if they are informed about them.

How much money is lost to public exchequer by way of false T.A. or per diem claims? How much money is lost by way of misuse of government vehicles? How much manpower, time and energy is lost by way of hoarding of files which the bureaucrats call lightly by the word "red - tapism?". How much money is lost to people by way of bribery and corruption? How do the police prevent them? The police do prevent them! The police do not think that they are crimes which they must prevent and control. The policeman is ignorant of the damages caused by such crimes or if at all they know it, they keep silence or tolerate it.

Let us take the traditional crimes? How many rapes were prevented by police? Sometimes, custodial rapes take place in police stations and actions are taken against such crimes. Could the actions taken so far prevent custodial rapes? Yes, they could. There is no accurate account of the number of rapes prevented by police by their control mechanisms/preventive strategies. Arm-chair speculations may argue that the rapes are controlled because the police are active in preventing them. How many kidnappings/abductions were prevented by police? How many forgeries were prevented by police? How many thefts were prevented by police? There is no answer to such questions although the police may claim that such crimes do not take place because the police keep a vigil on the occurrence of such crimes. There was a time when cattle thefts were plenty in the country.

Today, cattle thefts are not many or are non-xistent. Cattle thefts could be minimised because people understood that they were not profitable. It is not due to the police and their preventive works that cattle thefts were reduced. People do not want to commit cattle thefts because they can commit car thefts. Theft of motor vehicles are abnormally on the increase and there are gangs/ organized syndicates which encourage and patronize vehicle thefts. As automobile thefts are on the increase, the vehicle owners take precautions to see that their vehicles are not lost.

How many suicides are prevented by police? The dead bodies are seen on railway tracks, on water, in forests and are all of them suicides? Can the police control domestic violence? dowry harassment? — dowry deaths? What can the police do to prevent juvenile crimes? - abuse of children? - child labour? Of course the police can initiate actions against the employers of children and see that they are punished. But, can the police maintain millions of children employed in the country?. As far as the prevention of crimes which have social justice dimensions is concerned it is found that the preventive strategies of police have little or no impact. If at all there is some impact, it may be short run and the social problem it may cause may be something which the police can not control.

The police, we are told, was created by society for controlling and preventing crimes as well. This shows that the society wants the police to prevent crimes. In order to prevent crimes, they must collect the intelligence relating to the commission crimes. Do they collect such intelligence? Yes, they do - but, there is limitation. Many crimes are planned in a clandestine way and only a few come to the notice of the police. Plans for bomb explosions are sometimes unearthed by the intelligence wing of the police, but many explosions come to police notice only after the explosion. Intelligence on communal violence, political planning, student strikes, labour disputes etc.. may be collected by the police. Nevertheless how far does the intelligence so collected help the police to prevent crimes? The press sometimes speaks about the failure of police intelligence and if that is a truth, then it is necessary to make an indepth study about the effect of police intelligence in the prevention of crimes? Most unfortunately, such research wings are not at function in many police departments.

If the police are able to prevent crimes, it is doubtlessly a good thing. How many crimes are prevented by police? — are they able to prevent convictional crimes like Naxalism, Terrorism etc. Are they able to prevent crimes like custodial torture, concoction of evidence, manipulation of records and corruption in police? Are they able to prevent other enforcement crimes like hoarding of files, purposeful delay in investigation, perfunctory ways of investigation and miscarriage of justice? Are they able to prevent white collar crimes? Are they able to prevent disciplinary offences? Are they able to prevent offence under Special and Local Laws? There exists no data on the subject.

Objections to the Preventive Role of Police

The presence of police at a particular spot, certainly, prevents many crimes, often petty in nature, which have law and order implications and the effect continues so long as the police presence is ensured. They protect the V.I.P. at a trouble spot, control unruly crowds, engage in preventive patrolling, beat and surveillance. The obejections to the preventive role of police are:

1. Prevention of crime may be a police work. But the police may not be able to prevent many crimes as the causative factors of crime and criminal behaviour are beyond police control.

2. Many crimes which are committed by people are not reported to police. It means that the police do not know anything about many crimes that take place in society. If at all known, they don't always investigate them rather ignore them.

Ignorance about the occurrence of crimes and ignoring them are not prevention.

3. Police can not keep an eye on people - everywhere - on a permanent basis and therefore the police role in prevention of crime has only limited scope.

4. Many antisocial activities which the police must prevent are not crimes under law. Hence the police are helpless in such areas.

5. Where the police have been vigorous in taking preventive actions, empirical studies show that crimes are on the increase at other places where the police are not that vigorous.

6. Police under the pretext of preventing crimes do many things which are not justifiable. Sometimes, the police make use of their preventive powers to earn money or to encourage corruption.

7. Hardened criminals who are acquainted are not affected very much by the preventive strategies. They take precautions.

8. In offences where intense emotions are ingredients, the preventive strategies have no impact. How many crimes have been committed just in front of the police?

Thus, the objections are many against the police, yet the police claim that they have preventive roles. Here the police think that the people do not commit crimes because the police are there. Is it true to think so? Do their thinkings have any objective validity? People commit crimes in front of police and in spite of police! If that is the truth, how can the police claim that they prevent crimes in society? They can just say that they take preventive steps and they do not know how effective they are in really preventing crimes. To police,the effects of police strategies for preventing crimes may seem good, while to the people they may seem ineffective or useless. Therefore one can not really decide whether the preventive strategies of police are really effective without investigating the question whether the police itself is effective in their many areas of work. In spite of the police, the crimes are on the increase; in spite of many preventive steps initiated and enforced, the crimes of various categories are on the increase; in spite of serious investigation of crimes, many cases end in acquittals, in spite of many controls, the enforcement crimes show a rising trend and in such situations, the policemen themselves must answer: "how effective are the police in their preventive strategies?".

To be or not to be a policeman is not the issue under discussion. ":Why I am or I am not a Policeman"? - this needs an answer and the answer can be given only if the policeman in uniform is effective in his various tasks which he must perform in a human rights friendly way. When he thinks about preventing crimes, he thinks about the source crimes and surface crimes. Blade Companies — which is otherwise called financial institutions which offer exorbitant interest rate to investors and which accept highly exorbitant rate of interest from the lonees — advance money to people for purchasing automobile vehicles. After accepting the vehicle loan, some of them do not pay the principal and interest. In order to collect the loaned amount from them, these blade companies have "goondas" who by force and threatenings get the vehicle back/money back. Here, the goondaism may be only a surface crime and conduct of the blade companies is the source crime. The police can not prevent the working of the blade companies and logically it follows that the goondaism too can not be prevented by police so long as blade companies persist in society. I understand that goondaism becomes a way of life for some and an income generating source. Many goondas may not be goondas in the conventional meaning of the word, yet they pretend to be goondas to make a living and thereby a culture of goondaism develops in society. Goondas are necessary for many gang operators, for smugglers and even for people who want to threaten witnesses in criminal cases and thereby to get acquittal verdicts from the courts of law. The witnesses to crime may not even speak out the impact of goondas on their change of attitudes when they give testimony in courts.

Donations to get admissions in schools and educational institutions, commissions to many in clandastine contracts in business transactions, consultation fees to government doctors, corruption money for appointments, black money, N.O.C. rackets, VISA frauds, pickpocketing of patients in hospitals and clients by lawyers, carismatic and prayer frauds by religious men, flesh trade and sex-work etc...are seen in society. These crimes may have many side-crimes and the people may see only the side-crimes which flow from the invisible, but strongly perceived main crimes in society. Do the police prevent the principal (main) crimes or the visible side-crimes? Often the police may not be able to do both.

When political leaders who are in the hit - list move around, one may see armed police personnel around them with a purpose to prevent attacks on them. It is a constant and strong vigil and that alone can prevent attacks on the politician. In society too, such constant and strong vigil may be necessary to prevent crimes and, more often than not resultantly the police may not be able to do so and resultantly, crimes show an increasing trend. I do not know how far or how much did the police succeed in preventing crimes in the British past or even earlier. As a criminologist, now I can say that police alone will not be able to prevent any crimes, even if one forgets the incapability of police to prevent crimes which have international net work and intelligent execution. There is no remedy for any crimes although some temporary relief can be offered by a policeman.

Soul of Police Works

Many do not seem to have enough knowledge as to what exactly are the police works. Of course, the police Acts say somethings and the politicians speak quite different things. The policeman himself makes his own decisions and the departmental superiors say quite different things about what exactly are the duties of policemen? Is prevention of crimes more important than investigation of crimes?. At times, both may not be important as someone puts: "In police, what is very important is to become the blue eyed son of somebody who matters a lot in decision makings/in political hierarcy".

What is the soul of police work? I may propose that the soul of police work is administration of *just justice* by being a *public servant* being and not a government servant. Police may be administering 'justice' to people but one doubts whether or not they do it justly. *Police Justice* — i.e., justice as it is administered by police - is something the people do not sometimes approve of. In India, though *Police justice* has been developed, one does not find the development of something called the '*Police Ethics*'. Of course, an attempt was made for developing police ethics in the recent past. But, somehow or other it was not serious. People of questionable integrity and notorious character too administer *police justice*. The people do not and can not think that a simple thief is worse than a corrupt police officer who accepts bribe/ manipulates records to administer police justice. The police officer in such instances, probably, does more harm to the society than a person who committs pocket-picking or simple theft.

I do not know how the police administered police justice to people in the British past, but I understand that the police were not influenced by corrupt politicians then. As India was not a democracy then, the politicians had no scope at all at that time to go to police stations. How can a corrupt politician interfere in a just manner in police work? How can just police officer do things as influenced by the politician? The people will never regard the police as just if they understand that the police are vulnerable to political influence or corrupt practices. Hence police service to people will be regarded as disservice to them. This happens so because the police are yet to know the soul of police work. Police must be legal as well as moral in their administration of justice. Some police officers separate them and there starts the decay of police service to people. *Individualism* must not overpower justice consciousness.

Intolerance, Freedom and Righteousness in Police

Should the police tolerate crimes in society? Of course, omission to prevent crimes too is an offence in India and for a police officer, it is more than a crime. If F.I.Rs are going to be registered for the offences that take place in police stations — say, use of third degree methods to acceptance of bribe — I do not know how many F.I.Rs may have to be prepared! Do the policemen, police officers and the hierarcy show an attitude of tolerance or intolerance to such crimes — enforcement crimes— that take place under their nose or in front of their eyes? How can they prevent crimes in society if they are unable to prevent crimes that take place in police service or in the vicinity of police stations? Can we say that the misappropriation of secret service fund or claiming of false T.A. as offences? If so, what is the tolerance level of police officers and men to such malpractices? Some people simply refuse to go to police stations to register simple cases of theft, pocket-picking, simple hurt etc.., for, they are afraid that the expenses they have to bear may be more than what they suffer from the crime. Intolerance to the crimes committed by other people may be seen — but to the crimes committed by selves and/or colleagues may not be there. Such people can not prevent crimes in society as their vulnerability level to temptations and influences may be very high.

Nobody today believes that crimes do not take place in society, because the police are able to prevent them. Nobody today thinks that the police make attempts to prevent crimes because they are intolerant to crimes and criminals. People are inclined to think that crimes take place in all walks of life and in every sphere of human transactions. There are criminals in society just like there are criminals in police. In a world of criminals, there is no meaning in making attempts to locate and pinpoint criminals. Hence, be human rights friendly to all sorts of criminals.

Classical school of criminology brought the doctrine of free will to explain criminal behaviour and the Indian Penal Code 1860 was drafted following the doctrine. As sociology of crime, psychology of crime, endocrinology of crime, multiple causation approach, cultural theories, ecological explantions of criminal behaviour etc.. got developed, the doctrine of free will had a natural death. Law enforcement officers and the justice system believed the doctrine and made attempts to investigate crimes, prevent crimes and punish the criminals on the basis of the freedom of will. Necessarily, the approaches did not yield results either in eliminating crimes or curtailing their extent. Today, it is proved that the commission of crimes falls outside the sphere of any possible free will. I, for one, think that the police may be able to prevent crimes only if they understand the scientific explanations relating to the etiological factors in criminal behaviour. Any attempt to prevent crimes without making an earnest effort to eradicate the source from which crimes come up may be an exercise in futility. Police must be open to these facts before they initiate preventive strategies to the commission of crimes by people within and outside the police department. The free-will doctrine of crime causation remains just where it was. Whatever might have been thought about the free-will doctrine of crimes by St.Thomas Acquinas, Bentham and Beccaria as an explanation of sins and crimes, it is now quite clear that no criminologist believes in it in reality. It is possible to understand the causes of crime and the preventive steps taken by police must be with an intention to eradicate the sources of crimes rather than the crimes themselves. Slum life, poverty, affluence, mental disorders, defective ego formation, social structure, social processes, endoctrine malfunctionings, influence of media etc.. will have certain effects on a man's behaviours including criminal behaviour. The advocates of free will, law enforcement agencies and the justice system, unfortunately maintain still that a man can by his will power avoid committing crimes. They do not think that the why aspects of criminal behaviour are more important than the what aspects of crimes. Through preventive strategies, the police make attempts to prevent the what aspects and that is the precise reason why the police are unable to prevent crimes in spite of their attempts. Any police officer who has ever had to do something with crime - doers knows that a criminal commits crime owing to factors and forces which are within and outside his control. Whenever a man commits a crime, a police officer thinks that he is a criminal and he refuses to look into the etiological factors of his criminal behaviour.

Once a suspect was interrogated by the help of a polygraph. The polygraph refused to show correct markings. When the polygraph did not work well, the interrogator did not attribute its behaviour to the wilful refusal of the machine to cooperate with the interrogator. He called a technician and asked him to find out the defects and to set it right. When a suspect refused to give the responses in the way a police interrogator wanted him to give, he was tortured and thus made him to make a confession. The police interrogator thus committed a crime to prove a crime. There might be many reasons for his refusal to make a confession. The investigator did not bother about them. He thought that his commission of crime on the suspect was a method of proving the crimes and thereby preventing further crimes by himself and by others. Experience proves that commission of crimes does not prevent crimes in society. Prevention of crimes can be ensured only by scientific methods initiated by the participation of people. Torturing criminals or flogging crime-doers can not prevent crimes in society. Some police officers still believe that deterrence can prevent crimes. Yes, it may help preventing crimes to a certain extent — but limited only to certain types of crimes—only to such time the deterrence works powerfully in society. The moment deterrence is found inoperative, crimes may be again committed.

But, a deterrent police force ceases to be the friends of people. They are viewed as tormentors and are treated as a burden to society.

What is right and what is wrong in police? This needs discussion as people say that the police conception or righteousness is sometimes socially unacceptable in many ways—first and foremost in their lack of understanding of what is crime in society. They are taught at the police training centres that a crime is a violation of penal laws of the State. Take, for example, a man beats another and there he commits a crime. F.I.R. is registered against the crime-doer. He is brought to police station. He is manhandled inside the station. It is custodial torture and certainly is a crime. But here no F.I.R. is registered by anybody. Why? The double standard in approaches to the same acts-both being violations of the Penal laws — is objectionable to the public. The society thinks that crimes in society must be prevented and the crimes here mean the crimes within and outside the police stations. The righteousness of the police may say that the criminal acts of the people alone are crimes and with such an attitude the police will not be able to prevent crimes in society. A police officer/ man must maintain that the custodial crimes are more criminal than the crimes people commit in society.

Secondly, the police think that the people approve of police concepts of righteousness when people are convicted by courts. In reality, how many people in society hold the view that the police administer *just justice* to people? When convicted, do the people think that the police do everything in the *right way* for the conviction of the crime-doers? If not, the police concepts of righteousness is of questionable nature to the public. When acquitted, do the people think that the police do everything in the right way? Their concept of righteousness fail in courts? If not, there too, the police concepts of righteousness is of questionable nature.

How do the intolerance, freedom and righteousness in police help to prevent crimes in society?

Police and Control of Crimes under an Equal Justice System

Equal Justice System — I have discussed this in many of my books. This is a time people want *'distributive justice'* and the police may have to design their strategies in such a way that they must ensure equal justice under law. How should the police prevent crimes? A few guidelines are given below:

1. Accept the fact that the police are not the major agency to prevent various types of crimes in society. The police have only a limited role to play for preventing many types of crimes and even in those crimes which they may prevent, they can prevent them only temporarily and to a limited extent. Try to prevent crimes by ensuring people's participation and cooperation.

2. Educate the people as to how they must protect their person and property. For, individuals can protect themselves better than anybody else. The role of individuals, family, neighbourhood, community and society in preventing crimes against person and property — against themselves and others - must be taught to them. Police have an instructional role (as an educator) more than a preventive role in crimes in society. Assumption that the police are the principal crime prevention agency is false and causes irrepairable damages to public trust on police.

3. Prevent first all sorts of crimes the police commit — crimes of corruption, bribery, torture etc. — before they prevent people's crimes in society. A preventer of crimes should never be a crime-doer. People lose their trust on police when they see police committing crimes against them and in front of them. People in such situations may say: "Physician, cure thyself".

4. Ignorance of police on many crimes which cause serious harm to society — rupture in social stability and economic

growth - make many IPC crimes to be committed by people. Source crimes must be identified before surface crimes are checked and prevented. "Lice are caught when elephants are left free" - approach is harmful. Acts which were treated as crimes in 1860 when the Indian Penal Code was drafted are not the crimes that take place in 2000 A.D. Concepts, modalities, attitudes, approaches etc. have undergone changes and yet the police go after preventing traditional crimes. They, as a result, fail to prevent both types of crimes-traditional and current.

5. Making people aware about the new types of crimes by police may be the best preventive method. Many crime syndicates and investment racketeerings were prevented from their operations by police tactics. The police must therefore make extensive use of the media towards this end - in making public awareness of what is going on around them.

6. Police may be able to manage law and order situations, crime investigation or law and order crimes. Nevertheless, they may not be able to prevent many crimes which take place behind them or far away from their visibility. The "Quantum of Crimes" theory upholds that a certain quota of crimes — not less; not more — do take place in any society. Hence, the preventive strategies of police have only limited scope.

7. It is empirically demonstrated that more than ninety per cent of the crimes that take place in a society are not even known to police. If that is true, how can the police prevent crimes even when they are incapable of knowing the crimes that take place in society? Hence, prevention of crime by police may remain as a wishful thinking.

8. People who have decided to commit a crime do commit it even if the police keep a vigil on their activities. Police strategies for prevention of crime have no impact upon people who have determined to commit crimes. Such

criminals are not a few in any society. Convicted prisoners, sometimes, commit crimes when the prison officials look at them.

9. There is no statistical data to show how much or how many crimes are prevented by police every year. At the same time, there is enough proof to show that the crimes are on the increase. This is seen when the number of police personnel is increased over the years. The increased strength of police has not helped to put down crimes, but certainly has helped to detect more and more criminals. The more is the strength of police, the more will be the detection.

10. Police have many functions. Among them, what is the priority which is given to prevention of crime by police? Police collect intelligence — particularly that which relates to political fields. How much intelligence connected with crime is collected by police? It is said that prevention of crime and collection of intelligence relating to the prevention of crime receive only a law priority in police work. If that is true, it means that the police admit of their inability in preventing crimes to the extent the criticism goes.

11. Human rights are well recognised in India now. The awareness of human rights among the people create several barriers for the police to continue their crime-prevention works. Some of the old and older strategies of police are not forcefully enforced now. The directives of the Supreme Court of India (Cf. D.K. Basu V. State of West Bengal) create many problems for taking people or potential criminals into custody without respecting their human rights. Police complain that they are very much handicapped and handcuffed in their work towards prevention of crimes. This necessitates the development of human rights friendly approaches in preventing crimes. Heavy compensations may be awarded by Human Rights Commission in cases where human rights violations take place even in the prevention of crimes.

12. Emergence of the new concepts of justice, such as just justice, equal justice, total justice etc.. creates further problems in preventing crimes by orthodox methods. Rule by causing terror and fear among people, I think, may not work in future. People in the past — or even today — were afraid of police. Undoubtedly, the people listened to and obeyed the police out of fear and a rule of terror was accepted by the police and the people. Today there is a growing awareness among the people that they are no longer "small" as they were viewed by the police in the past. They are the votes of the government in power — of the opposition which is equally powerful as the ruling government. When the police misbehave with people or cause fear and terror among the public for preventing crimes or in the pretext of preventing crimes, politicians, human rights activists, public litigation societies, civic minded people and so on take interest on people and their causes more than what they do for the police. The vote banks in a democracy want the police to be people friendly and in such a system, the police can not prevent crimes in the way they want.

Thus, I think that we have to recognize the changes in society and the changing role of police in a democracy. One can not function as a policeman unless he recognizes human dignity and individual's freedom even when he prevents the commission of crimes. A policeman who accepts his limitations can perform his functions better than the one who thinks that he has unlimited and unrestricted freedom and power to prevent crimes in society. A policeman is a man even when he prevents crime and he will be prevented from exercising his authority if he does not honour human rights and man's dignity.

3

Police Investigation of Crimes: What I Feel?

Investigation of crime is an important function of the police but it seems to me that it is given only a lower priority than law and order management. When the law and order is in trouble, the ruling government becomes disturbed and the opposition becomes more active. When crimes are acquitted and crime-doers escape punishment, the authorities do not become uneasy as they ought to be. Look at the conviction rate in the Country and in States. The conviction rate goes down and disappointingly it is frustratingly low in some States. Perhaps, crime investigation is the only work the police must do by themselves, for, the existing law empowers only the police to investigate crimes. Crime investigation was easier in the past, but today it is highly complicated, complex and needs exceptional ability and intelligence, integrity and enthusiasm, earnestness and energy. It was thought that crimes were of simple nature and could be proved by eye-witnesses. But today, the crimes are extremely complicated and intelligently executed by people who are, sometimes, experts and specialists in the commission of crimes. A police officer who has some police training in a general way for an year may be a poor investigator. It is alleged that every police officer is a generalist and he can not undertake jobs which specialists must do. I think that the allegation is not altogether baseless. Universities in the west offer Master's

Programme in police science and investigation and it lasts for two or three years. One year's police training includes only a few classes in investigation and police science and under any stretch of imagination, one can not say that the training provides adequate expertise to investigators. In a premier police training institution, I am told, there is no classes taken on police interrogation. The reason may be that there is no qualified member in the faculty to deal with such sensitive areas which require indepth knowledge about the working of the human psyche. I wrote a book 'Police Interrogation: Dos which the police do not Do" and I find that it may be the only scientific book on police interrogation in India—dealing elaborately on the subject. A retired police officer who was considered to be an expert interrogator was candid enough to tell me that he did not understand much by reading my book. He was honest enough to tell me that he lacked adequate education in psychology. He said that he was honoured as an effective interrogator by his colleagues in the department and the reason for his success, according to him, was his intuitive power and God's providence. But, many police interrogators may not be blessed with such powers and therefore it is meaningless to expect the help of such supernatural powers for all investigators.

Different crimes are of different nature and so are different types of criminals. Some of the most modern crimes are done by crime experts against whom the police can not apply any human rights unfriendly approaches. They are to be arrested as per the directives issued by the Supreme Court of India (Cf. D.K. Basu V. State of West Bengal) and have to be interrogated psychologically and scientifically. Jame's Law is a psychological principle applied by an interrogator during his interaction with the interrogated. How many police officers have heard about such a law? — I do not know. Yet, I can say that many do not have any scientific knowledge about the working of defence mechanisms in suspects/interrogators during the process and progress of interrogation. Defence mechanisms are the basis on which Jame's Law operates.

Probably, police officers still hold the view that crime investigation is something which they can conduct without bothering much about the after effects. Today, a situation has come into being that the accused acquitted by courts of law make claims for victimological compensation for what they suffered during the process and progress of investigation. Police investigators have accountability and have to pay compensation to the victims of the misuse of power/abuse of authority. Third millennium police will have to face this problem, doubtlessly, I feel, in a more severe way than what they see at present.

If police investigators have to face problems, then naturally they may show reluctance to take up investigation work. I am told by some police investigators, just a few days ago, that the development of the concepts of victim justice, human rights justice,. equal justice etc.. make them to avoid investigation work. Unless something positively is done to make crime investigation very scientific, it may be difficult for them to take up the job. Specialists are necessary and specialized investigation becomes very essential. Investigation conducted in cases of ordinary murder may be useless when it comes to the investigation of a calculated and pre-planned murder. Some crimes have inter-state and international ramifications and precisely therefore they will be highly complicated and complex. The strategies of investigation which were used a decade back may be of no utility now when people make use of cell-phones, e-mails and computers.

Equal Justice and Police Investigation

Justice is and should be distributive - '*equally or as far as possible equally*' - to all deserving justice in a criminal case. A number of people suffer and the investigation is intended to offer justice to all. Till yesterday, police thought that they conducted investigation to administer justice to the criminals against whom the society had a retributive or vindictive attitude. Punishing the criminals alone does not satisfy the people today. They want victim justice and human rights justice. They want the police to honour the concepts contained in just *justice* administration and in such a system, every suspect is considered as a man of dignity. The police have to investigate crimes respecting human dignity and precisely therefore the old methods of investigating crimes become unacceptable. Detaining the suspects for several days in police custody incommunicado might have yielded good results in the past, but today it may result in an inquiry conducted by the Human Rights Commission for awarding compensation to the suspect who becomes a victim of abuse of power/misuse of authority. In a system that demands transparency, illegal detention of suspects incommunicado in police custody becomes difficult, if not impossible. A policeman in the past could do so with certain amount of immunity as the people were not courageous enough to insist transparency in police work. A lot of stories were heard about such illegal detentions during the internal emergency (1976-77) in India, but today things have changed a lot.

Equal justice system insists just justice to the crime-doer, to the victims of crime/abuse or misuse of authority and power, to the society and to the justice system itself. I have dealt with this at length in my previous books. Justice to the criminal means just investigation in a just justice system. Investigation is not an exercise to punish the guilty in any way - it must be to convict the crime-doer in a just way, by just means and through just methods. Conviction for what? Criminologists may say that the conviction is for correction and not for destruction of the convicted. Investigation and incareeration must be seen only from such perspectives. But, many policemen see investigation only from his narrow perspectives and therefore he can not see a corrected criminal at the end of the process of justice investigation. Police officers with such narrow vision may use any unauthorized methods to see that the accused is convicted. This is against the principles of an equal justice system.

Police is a subsystem in justice administration and is viewed only as a part of the whole system aimed to administer just justice to all including crime-doers and hard-core criminals. Crime-doers and hard-core criminals have a lot of rights which must be recognised by police, prosecutors and courts. There are people who still hold the view that any suspect will confess his crime, if he is tortured. To me, their arguments are not convincing and it seems prudent to suppose that they are mistaken. In spite of the crude approaches and torture methods, the conviction rate could not go up beyond 50 per cent at the national level. The figure relates only to those cases charge-sheeted after detection. The percentage of detection is deplorably low in some States and if that is the truth, then the theories of confession by torture or investigation by unauthorized means and methods become useless even for academic discussion or foot path sales. What the people thought as "success" was only "failure" and that is the main reason why people insist for scientific and psychological investigation.

Crime Investigation During Ancient Times

Crimes have been committed by people from time immemorial - ever since man came to the world. Crimes have been investigated by some means or methods ever since and punishments awarded. Society found that the means and methods adopted by people to investigate crimes and to administer justice were not just and effective. Hence the society gave birth to organized police system and entrusted the work of investigation to police officers who were trained for the purpose. In India one could see the police using torture methods. (Cf. Torture Commission - 1855) even during the inception of the organized policing till yesterday (See the reports of the Amnesty International and news in the press) and in such a setup, it becomes very necessary to convince the people that the police are scientific and psychological in investigation works. The policemen felt pleasant to be the investigators of crime, for, it conferred power and authority to them. For the people, it was not pleasant. For, they found the police employing crude and sometimes inhuman methods for investigating crimes. In spite of them, a large number of cases got acquitted. I do not think that the police alone must be responsible for the large scale acquittals.The police depended upon witnesses who often gave different versions to police and to the courts. The Evidence Act favoured it and resultantly scientific evidence did not get due importance in court proceedings I do not think that scientific evidence can prove everything against an accused in a crime. Nevertheless, it can help a lot. Oral testimony of eye-witnesses will prove many things and scientific evidence will prove many more things which witnesses may not be able to prove. Due emphasis and importance must be given to both. The ignorance of lawyers, prosecutors, presiding officers, probably, makes the investigating officers not to depend heavily on scientific evidence.

'Police interrogator' — this is a new concept for Indian police. The police still think that anybody can be a police interrogator. They still hold the view that police interrogation can start at any time — even without any reliable evidence collected against the suspect in the crime. Interrogate the suspect and collect evidence' — this approach seems to dominate police interrogator. If this is the position, I think that there is no difference between crime investigation conducted by lay people in ancient times and by police officers in the present days. Whatever that be, specially trained crime - interrogators become a necessity under an Equal Justice System which honours human rights justice to suspects under interrogation.

Police Investigation and Philosophy Behind

'Why I am a Policeman?'-a policeman asks to himself and he answers the question as : "I am a policeman not to do everything during the process and progress of investigation. I am to do only limited things and I must not venture to do anything for which I am not professionally competent and qualitatively suitable". Criminals too are part of the society and the conditions/factors which etiologically responsible for their commission of crimes or for their involvement in the commission of crimes are discoverable provided an honest policeman wants them to be brought out. Arrest, bail, remand, prosecution, trial and they are not everything in administration of justice. There is a purpose for everything and a philosophy for each one of them. I think that a lack of knowledge about the purpose and philosophy behind crime investigation may have made the situation as it is seen today. People are skeptical about the success of investigation by ordinary policemen. They want specialized crime investigation team or the Central Bureau of Investigation to conduct investigation even in petty thefts and simple hurts. Why? It is rational to suppose that public trust ceases when quality of investigation ceases to exist. Crimes are human acts and people may continue to commit crimes. Effective investigation is a method to control crimes and logically it follows that defective investigation may work as an incentive to crime-prone people in society.

Investigation of crime is not only for administering criminal justice through conviction by a court of law in genuine cases in which the accused is guilty, but also for administering justice to the victims of crime as well as to the victims of abuse of power and authority. After investigation, if an innocent person is charge-sheeted and subsequently acquitted by the court, then the acquitted, in all fairness, deserves justice by way of compensation. The investigators are not meant for miscarriage of justice. Many argue for a total justice system - a just justice system and an equal justice system. If so, it is necessary that investigation must be just and total in every respect.

Fear of policemen, individually or collectively, dominates much of the crime-doer's mind and thinking. He knows that many things the police investigate against him will land him into jail. Hence, he may create barriers on the investigators path to success. He may try to win over police witnesses or may go to the extent or bribing the investigator/prosecutor. Investigators must be beyond reproach and if investigation is perfect then justice will flow automatically in majority of cases. The crime - doers will be administered justice and that is what the people want now.

Investigation of crime is an attempt to control crimes and administer just justice under an equal justice system. If the investigation is done by unqualified or underqualified police investigators and the police investigators can be controlled by departmental and extradepartmental forces, pressures and temptations etc.. then the people may not require such a system to administer justice. Allegations are plenty blaming the investigating officers becoming vulnerable to pressures and pleasantness. There are studies too proving the allegations. In former days, people tolerated it and continued to invest money to maintain the system. But, now? People say that the police are accountable to what they do. Miracles do not happen in police work and the people too do not want miracles to happen during investigation. At the same time, they want proper return to their investment and I think that the public demand for an enviable output from police investigation will be more in the years to come.

Belief in police earnestness and efficiency must not be allowed to diminish and the only option to remedy the situation is to employ honest investigators who have qualitative expertise. People feared the police in the past and they still fear the police. I feel that all types of fears are bad. When more and more investigations become failures, the people start to feel contempt for the police system. The fear turns out to be hopelessness and this sort of hopelessness keeps the people away from police. People may not report crimes to police, for, they do not have any hope that justice will be done.

Who is a Good Policeman?

Some say that an honest policeman who is less efficient is always better than a corrupt policeman who is very effective. Some others say that a corrupt policeman who is efficient is always better than an honest and inefficient policeman. I do not know what they mean by honesty, efficiency and corruption etc... Yet, I may say that values are values in police service too. Hence, a value-oriented investigation is always appreciated and desired by people. End does not justify the means and therefore it is necessary to cultivate values among the policemen. "Why I am not a policeman?" "I am not a policeman, for, I can not keep up my values if I wear the police uniform" — if such thoughts keep coming to the mind, then it is better to search for another job than sticking to a job which is not value based for him. Once a deputy inspector general of police, crime investigation, told his superintendent of police to parade the suspects in nude and the superintendent of police simply refused to do so. According to the superintendent, parading in nudeness is not a just means in administering just justice. What is right and what is wrong during an investigation? This is decided by some normative scales which are accepted by the legal system and the people. When helpless suspects in police lockups committed suicide, some police officers insisted that the suspects might be kept in nakedness in police custodial facility. They found some relationship between clothes one had and the suicide he committed. For many in police lockups committed suicide by hanging for which they used their long dothi. When some were locked up, then their clothes were not removed. Why? What happened to the theory that the clothes made people to commit suicides in police lockups? Even when male detinues were kept in nakedness in police lockups,? still some of the detainees committed suicide. Why? A value based investigator should not think of such human rights violations for administering justice or in the pretext of administering justice. Informal arrests, illegal detentions, concoction of evidence, manipulation of records, use of third degree methods, employment of tutored witnesses, suppression of facts, suggestion of falsehood, corruption and corrupt practices, vulnerability to unjust influences etc.. have never earned a name or reputation for any police investigator. Such things will never make investigation envitable and the result in such type of investigation will be miscarriage of justice and supreme dishonour to the people who maintain the system.

Though justice is administered by the legal system - or - is supposed to be administered, a value based justice only will survive. For values are more fundamental than all other things in justice administration. If a policeman does not have values in life, then the justice he administers will also be devoid of values. A director general of police who occupies the top position and who does not have values in life will be treated as a mean person by people whereas a police constable who is at the bottom most position of the department will be respected if he possesses values in investigation. In India, deterioration has come into being at the top level of police administration and that is what is being shown in films and T.V serials in these days. Bureaucrats - politicians - businessmen nexus makes matters worse now than what they were in the past. People think: "What justice can come from the police when the top level is rotten?". "Show me the supervisors in police department, then I shall tell you what type of investigation you will do to administer justice" — said once a research scholar to me. Yes, I think that there was a strong point in what he said. For, I notice that the conviction and acquittal rates vary depending upon superiors in the investigation units. People demand certain officers to be posted in crime investigation units and certain others in law and order management. Why?

Justice is a word which covers a variety of feeling for the people. Roughing up the suspects by the policeman may be justice for some; humiliating the suspects may be justice for others. Refusing bail to the suspects may be justice for a third group and compelling the suspects to remain in semi-starved/starved condition may be justice for a fourth group. Vested interests may interpret justice in the way they want and the police investigators are not intended to dance according to the tunes of the vested interests. Nevertheless, allegations are heard that some investigators yield themselves to vested interests — may be communalism, corruption, affiliation, inlfuence etc.. They infact do a great disservice to people and humanity. People ask: "Why so many cases end in acquittals if the police investigators are not yielding themselves to vested interests?". I have no answer to their questions, yet I may say that facts may be sometimes stranger than fiction.

If investigation does not guarantee justice, then it offers miscarriage of justice or injustice. Both are in a way opposite to justice. I do not know how many people have gone to jails by miscarriage of justice or by injustice. In any case, people who have been fined (as a penalty) are certainly more than those who are imprisoned. One can not simply deny the fact that a few people could have been executed by miscarriage of justice or by injustice administration. Probably, those who could have been punished for life sentence would be more than those who were given capital punishment. Researches have proved that a certain percentage of the inmates in any penal institutions were innocent ones.

In acquittals, I have discussed in detail in my earlier books, how does miscarriage of justice/injustice take place. I do not want to repeat my observations here. In any case, the more are the acquittals, the more are the number of defective and perfunctory investigation for which the police are certainly accountable. In the name of justice, innocent people are convicted and in the same name, the guilty are acquitted. And I do not know how can I call it to be justice administration? "*Let one thousand criminals go unpunished, no innocent one must be punished*" — this is not justice administration whatever may be the arguments on that count. Justice administered basing on such dictums of jurisprudence does not mean much to me. The dictum should be, as I have pointed out in my earlier writings, that all the guilty must be punished and the innocent must be set free. The innocent in such situations must get victimological compensation for the sufferings they undergo for fighting against the mammoth justice administration agencies. I emphasise that justice will be full and just only if it ensures total justice to the criminals, to the victims, to the society and to the justice system itself under an equal justice administration.

When, after an investigation, an innocent person is charge-sheeted it is called an atrocity committed on a helpless man and when he is acquitted as found innocent, it is not called benevolence or charity done to him. He must go unpunished, but must get victimological compensation as well. How many false cases are registered? — I do not have data in my hand. But I have research evidence to show that courts have acquitted the accused as the cases were false or as the accused were totally innocent. If the acts of investigators in such types of cases are to be called by proper names I sincerely confess that I do not have a *proper word* to describe such '*administration of justice*'.

Justice at its fullest is an indissoluble combination of many kinds of justices — normally, investigative justice, human rights justice, gender justice, just justice, prosecuting justice, trial justice, victim justice etc... The pleasure of the society in a just justice administration lies in seeing that all sorts of justices are administered to all affected by the commission of crime. If the investigation is defective, it affects all kinds of justices offered thereafter. Why should the society invest so much money on police if they do not investigate crimes properly? — ask some civic minded people in society. According to them, the investment becomes a waste.

I do not want to write anything ask to how we can or how we must improve our police investigation. For, I have written enough on the subject. Still, I wish that something must be done to improve the training of police officers/men in making expert police interrogators and in changing police attitude to witnesses and to the public. I firmly think that the police - witness relationship must not come to an end when the witness statement is recorded. It must continue till the case is disposed off and afterwards. When crimes are convicted, the press reports them as if something unusal has taken place. The convictions in criminal cases have news value and the acquittals do not have so much news value as the convictions have? Is it because the acquittals are common and convictions are rare? What is the meaning of publishing the photographs of the prosecutors and police officers when criminal cases of sensational nature are convicted? Investigation of criminal cases is the normal - usual - routine duty of police officers and success in their work should not become a news item in the media. But, it comes. Why? For, the press knows that success in investigation has news value now.

Investigation by Police, Defence Lawyers and Private Detective Agencies

There was a time crime investigation was the monopoly of the police. But, today lawyers do the same. I have got a couple of friends who studied criminology and foresic science along with me. They practice law in courts and often they appear for the defence. I met them a few days ago and they told me that they investigated crimes and thus they defeated the police. Going to the scene of crime, inspecting the scene of crime, conducting tests on scientific evidence etc.. are just a few things they do. Why do we think in this way? There are retired forensic experts who help the accused in their cases and for it they make use of their scientific expertise and tests. Some of them have a lot of work. Besides, there are private detective agencies undertaking investigative work in their own way. Investigative journalism is a developed branch now.

Yes, from the practical and utilitarian points of view, what is the advantage of convicting crime-doers at present? If fines are imposed, then the State is the beneficiary. But, expenses which the State incures to get a fine from the crime-doers is more than what the State gets by way of fine. By incarceration, the State bears the expenses to maintain the inmates in the prisons. Incarceration is meant for the correction of the inmates. But, how many inmates are corrected? The number of recidivists are going up and from that point of view, the incarceration does not yield enviable results. Guilty people who get acquitted adjust themselves in society and it goes, therefore, without saying that imprisonment is not necessary for the correction of crime-doers. Then why should we send the convicted to prisons? Thus there are many questions than answers and as such the people are confused about the utility or objective of punishment today. Hence, administration of justice basing on imposition of punishment to the crime-doers needs rethinking. A system that accepts distributive justice – total justice – only have survival value in the years to come.

Some investigators ask the question: "Why should we investigate the crimes to see that the crime-doers are punished?". If investigation of crime does not offer victim justice and public satisfaction, then such an investigation becomes meaningless and that is the reason why some investigators are not serious in their work. Justice has been today identified with the verdict of a court of law. I do not think that such a view is right. Acquittals and convictions have no meaning unless they ensure victim justice. The victims of crime are the sufferers in crime. And any acquittal or conviction which does not ensure justice to the victims of crime can not be treated as anything more than a process in justice administration. The acquittals and convictions in criminal cases must be tested by examining whether or not they tend to guarantee justice to all people affected by the commission of crime. For example, think of an individual who is acquitted by court. He spends a lot of money and suffers a lot to get an acquittal. After the acquittal, he continues to suffer financially, psychologically, socially etc.. and in such a case, what type of justice does the system offer to him? I have seen people who have become wrecks in life just because they happened to be the accused in criminal cases. Even after their acquittal, they continued to suffer. What type of justice has been offered to them? People may say: "The truth comes out at the end" and the question is "What is the use or earthly benefit if at all the truth has come out at the end?" In a sensational case, the suspects were tortured. They sold their property to fight against the system. They suffered mentally. There were humiliated. They became pauper in life and "sick in health". Ultimately, they were removed from the array of the accused.

What type of justice was that ? In another case, the accused were convicted for life. Their family members then said: "A life sentence for the accused means a life sentence for the entire family". They asked further: "Does the society have a responsibility to extend an assistance to the victims of such convictions?". The State has several plans to uplift the poor and the downtrodden, the sick and the disabled, the victimized and the handicapped and in such a welfare State, why not see the victims of convictions as human beings, handicapped and victimized by the State's action?

The victims of crime too advance similar arguments. Victims of crime are the sufferers in the crime and they must get justice first before anybody is administered justice. But, as things happen today, they are the most ignored lot and precisely therefore, they must be treated as victimised and handicapped. There is the immediate need to have a Victim Fund to look after them and Victim Compensation Tribunals must be established to offer justice to the victims of crime. I have dealt with this elaborately in some of my previous books.

Police Rules and Crime Investigation

Police have any number of rules to guide them during investigation of crimes. But, do they observe them always? Do they violate them? If they observe them meticulously, many of the evils seen today may not be there. If they violate them, then the law enforcers become the law violators. In that case, they do not have even the moral rights to be investigators. An interrogator wants to question a suspect. He knows the rules, but does not have the required expertise to interrogate the suspects. We think him unfit to interrogate the suspect if he adopts means and methods which are of a questionable nature. We think ill of such an interrogator even if he is able to extract a confession from the suspect. Some interrogators derived exquisite pleasure in inflicting torture on the suspects. No sensible man can praise such people even if they get success from their interrogation. A sense of *just justice* is a part of police interrogation. Scientific and psychological interrogation can give satisfaction to the justice system, to the society and to the individual suspects. This part of police morals plays a great part — or ought to play — in the training of police interrogators. An interrogation through torture is an act of passion and not of reason and of justice consciousness. Expertise and professionalism are better than knowledge in police rules, for, they bring satisfaction to many. Police rules have not always been faultless and that is the reason why the rules are sometimes amended. The law says that male witnesses can be called to police stations for recording their statements. Experience shows that the law is bad to get the willing cooperation of the witnesses. It being so, the individual investigators amend the law and go to the witnesses to conduct the interview with them.

I think that some of the current methods/strategies of investigation are a curious blend of utilitarianism and wrong notions of police power and authority which cause a police ego inflated with false status consciousness and pasted vanities. Perhaps the ego part has the stronger hold among some police interrogators. In olden days, the police ego had good effects upon the people, but today, owing to the growing awareness of human rights consciousness and limitations of police powers, the people are inclined to ignore the police ego to the extent possible. Resultantly, some people do not cooperate with the police while others show positive hostility to police ways of doing. Police officers say that the people do not cooperate with them because they have lack of civic consciousness and citizens' sense of responsibility. They fail to or refuse to think that civic consciousness does not grow in vacum and precisely therefore the police must create environments in which the people can express their civic consciousness. False ego projections and police vainglories have no place in scientific investigation of crimes. Police investigation becomes successful only with the support and co-operation of people. It is evident that a police officer with a scientific outlook and expertise in investigation can not let himself be intimidated by vanities and vainglories. He will not be prepared to say that investigation is a police baby, rather will say that it is a joint venture by police and people through science. He will inquire whether he will be able to ensure public's co-operation in his work. And, he will find total support of witnesses to prove the crime before a court of law. He will find also that his expertise and professionalism, like that of other experts in other areas, involve public appreciation of his work. The traditional methods of police interrogation are seldom accepted and appreciated by many people.

Let us take the investigation of a crime from its commission to its disposal and note the points where lack of expertise inflict preventable sufferings. I begin with the commission of crimes. Whatever may be the causative factors, the police are legally bound to investigate the crimes. The crime-doers know it well and therefore they make all attempts to escape detection. The success of a good investigator lies in the collection of evidence from all sources including a careful and scientific inspection of the scene of crime. The suspect must be arrested only after collection of evidence and he may be interrogated by bringing evidence against him. Muscles have no role in such interrogation. Evidence will speak louder than the interrogator and the entire exercise must be done psychologically and as per the procedure established by law. Science and scientific knowledge alone must guide the investigator. No suffering must be inflicted in the name of administering justice, but the sufferings which are logical and incidental to the legal procedure are always tolerated and appreciated. When the suspect is rich or influential, they have the best treatment. If the suspect is poor or does not enjoy the advantages of the influential or affluent, then they have the worst treatment. This, if happens, is not justice, it is then called miscarriage of justice. The investigating officers then are said to condemn the helpless and the handicapped. Yet, we may claim that justice is administered!

Crime Investigation Branch and Justice

I know that crime investigation branches are established to enable the investigators to give their full time attention to investigation of crimes which are entrusted to them. The officers working there claim that they are experts in the field of crime investigation. The popular belief is that a *criminal is afterall a criminal* and therefore he deserves punishment. Undoubtedly, the criminal commits certain acts which the society wants to prevent. Every crime proclaims to the world that the society fails to prevent crimes. If the society fails in preventing crimes, then the police investigates the crime for punishing the criminals. It is believed that the society prevents commission of crimes by punishing the criminals. Of course, I have a different view about the impact of punishment on prevention of crimes. I do not want to make any arguments to prove my views as they do not fall within the scope of this book. Any way, the crimes are investigated and how do the police investigate them? We may take murder as a case for our discussion. Society can not permit people to commit murders and therefore the murderer has to be punished and it should be done through a procedure established by law. Police are not empowered to investigate murder in the way they want. If they violate the laws, the society reacts to their behaviour. For, punishment to the murderer through established legal methods is permitted and any harm more than the punishment is wholly prohibited. The society does not take a vindictive approach to murderers although it used to be retributive to criminals in the past. It being so, the society does not allow the investigators/ police to be vindictive to murderers. For, vindictiveness to criminals, experience shows, could not so far lessen the number of crimes. By inflicting punishment on criminals, one can not totally eradicate crimes in society. Prevention of crime, investigation of crimes and punishment to criminals are three different things. For preventing crimes, police are not authorized to inflict pain on criminals under their custody. For punishing crimes, the police are not empowered to inflict pain on criminals. The police are legally required to investigate crimes in a lawful and just manner. I do not and I can not justify any cruelty or croocked practices by police during investigation of crimes. The special crime investigation team is established to ensure that the criminals get what is due to them by lawful procedures. Crimes and criminals exist in society irrespective of police taking actions against criminals and in spite of police investigating crimes. If that is so, be decent to crime-doers and dignified in police actions.

Police have muscle and power. They intoxicate people just like liquor does. But the effect of liquor lasts for a few hours and afterwards, man becomes normal. Power intoxicates a man so long as he enjoys the power. Power does not last longer and even powerful empires have perished. Powerful men have died, yet they live, even after their destruction or death as the case may be, through their acts and activities. Many police officers - veteran investigators of crimes–powerful men of authoirty unquestioned ruler in the jurisdiction–have served the police department and people before and after India became independent. For the last 23 years, I have seen many police officers of different descriptions, characters and personality traits. Some of them have retired and some of them have become sick or died. I see a few of them making a morning walk forlorn and forsaken by the very same people whom they have served once. I have listened to people making comments when they see the old and infirm police officers go for their morning walk and the comments were: "Decent, just, God-fearing, neat, cruel, unsympathetic, proud, corrupt, authoritarian, nastly, evil minded, barbarous, animal like" and I used to think that those comments speak a lot about the working of the police department after independence and even now. "Why I am not a Policeman?" - "I am not, because I do not want to be counted as one among those morning walkers". "Why I am a Policeman?"—"I am a policeman because I want to be decent, just and God-fearing in my service". Investigation of crime is an area where one can be what he wants to be and it can be anything from man-like to animal-like. What type of investigation one must conduct to offer fair and just justice to people under an Equal Justice System during third millennium must be decided by the individuals, the department and the society.

4

Law and Order: What I do not Understand?

I have certain concepts about "Law and Order" and I do not know whether or not my concepts of "Law and Order" coincide with the concepts of "Law and Order" which some in police still entertain in their mind. A police officer on his return from patrolling, writes in the vehicle book "Law and Order duty". There is no disorder in the law and order situation and the people live in harmony. Yet, he writes "Law and Order"duty. Can he not go to the people for "human conducts" amd establish good police- people relationship instead of going for *law and order duty* among people who live in harmony and happiness? *Perception* matters a lot and a change in perception makes a total change in police functionings among them. A police officer who goes with a perception to maintain law and order among people who live in peace and order may make attempts to see law and order violations everywhere. One may see a police patrolling party returning to police stations with people who (I do not know what crimes they commit) create law and order problems in the jurisdiction. Many people are taken into custody like that by the police and the Supreme Court recently gave some directives to police for observance when they would take people into custody. The concept of law and order changes now — and has already changed a lot from what it was earlier.

Indian Police Act - 1861 clearly lays down that if is the duty of police to maintain law and order. The Act does not speak in clear terms what is meant by '*Law and Order*'. Can we say that a country where people found to look down upon people on the basis of castes/sub-caste maintains law and order? I do not think that the police can see to it that casteism is abolished or if they can do so, certainly they can easily maintain law and order. Perhaps, the law and order contemplated by the Indian Police Act did not mean this sort of a law and order - i.e., a casteless society. So long as a number of castes and sub-castes exists in society, a certain number of caste conflicts is bound to occur. Can the police name them as law and order problem? Or, should they look at them as the inevitable outcome of a caste-ridden society? Can arrests and actions under the Indian Penal Code-1860,or any other special and local laws find a remedy/ relief to the caste conflicts? The problem is more a communal issue than a law and order issue. The law and order issue, as the police may call it, is not a police problem to be solved by lathies, rifles and tear gas shells. Persuation, appeal and negotiation may solve the issues better than police tactics and strategies.

A communal problem may be a law and order problem and to that extent, I can understand the patrol-man writing in his diary as "Patrol duty for law and order maintenance". I can also understand him taking some people into custody during his patrol duty and not at all the usual patrol-man returning with people everyday after his usual patrol duty. Allegations are heard that the patrol party questions many on roads and take some of them to police stations and make them suspects/accused in crimes which, more often than not, are not real. A public prosecutor once told that some of the people brought by police as "goondas" or burglers and so on were not "goondas" and burglers. They could be homeless people, street sleepers, odd-time passengers and so on.

A lot of misconceptions exist in police about the concept of law and order. Corruption-Mafia is a law and order problem and I may argue that the whole law and order in the society will be disturbed if corruption becomes rampant in society. How can a corrupt administration ensure law and order in society? A corrupt man does not have respect for law and a man who has no respect for law can never maintain order in his jurisdiction. Indian Police Act-1861 which entrusted law and order maintenance to police did not think that the root cause of many law and order problems was corruption-in society in politics - in bureaucracy-in police-in administration. I am told that once there were serious law and order problems in educational institutions causing heavy damages to public property and the police had to interfere in many places. It was alleged that the root cause of the agitation was the corruption by a political party which handled the 'education portfolio' then. Behind every serious law and order issue, one can find corruption and corrupt elements playing many roles.

Hoarding, blackmarketing, adulteration etc.. cause law and order problems. How? They disrupt the society's balance and the disruption in the social balance will cause many law and order issues. How many hartals, *bandhs* and mass agitations have been organized in India to bring down the prices of essential commodities? And in such hartals/*bandhs*, a lot of law and order problems emerge and the police tackle them in many ways including the use of muscle powers.

I do not know how far will the police be able to maintain law and order, if the forces which operate for causing law and order violations are beyond the control of police? Certainly, I have no doubt that the police will be able to give a temporary relief in any law and order situation and the relief may relate to the control of violence at the area of disturbance. So long as the causes of disturbance exist there, the police can remain there to act as a force to put down crimes of violence.

It is a basic principle in criminology that a crime-doer alone can prevent crimes in society and for that purpose, he should decide not to commit crimes. Deterrence or causing of fear may stop crimes so long as they exist in society and the police cause fear and terror at a scene of law and order disturbance. Like an allopathic medicine, it works well for the time being for a quick relief, but a permanent solution to law and order issues must be found out through other means. In that way the police are just an agency for a sudden and quick action at law and order situations. Instances are plenty to show that law and order crimes do take place in spite of and in front of police at the scene of disturbance.

Investigation of crime is something which the police alone can do and for the success of it, they require public help and willing participation. I have talked about it earlier. The management of law and order becomes a police baby only when disturbance at the scene necessitates immediate police intervention. Suppression of the problem by the iron hands of police may be necessary. The real management of law and order lies with the people, particularly with those who act as the cause of law and order disturbance. Any number of examples can be pointed out to show how active are some of the relgious fundamentalists and communal fanatics in creating law and order problems. What can or what should the police do in such situations? I have come across some people who told me during communal violence that some police action could aggrevate the disturbance beyond control. They wanted the police to use rifles, lathies and tear gas shells to aggrevate the situation. They wanted the police to conduct house to house searches for taking people into custody. They knew that such police strategies would further complicate the issue. In that way police action at a scene of law and order management must be carefully structured so that police actions themselves do not cause further law and order complications.

Politicians play very important role in creating law and order situations and in solving the issues they thus create. Policemen encourage, discourage or become indifferent depending upon the political backing of the law and order disturbance. Anything can be a cause of law and order disturbance and it depends upon how the politicians interpret the issue. Politically instigated students caused once serious law and order problems at the university headquarters for nearly three years and the disturbance continued until the politicians who instigated the students to do it asked them to withdraw from it. Politicians claim that they do it for a noble purpose in society and it is an accepted way in a democracy. If the opposition to the ruling front keeps silence, then it meets with a natural death. It being so, law and order disturbance caused by the political parties become a necessary evil in a democratic setup. What can the police do if politicians cause law and order disturbance? I propose that the police should keep maximum restraint in such situations particularly when they use force against the agitating masses of people. Police are accountable to what they do at a law and order disturbance in such situations. After a law and order management, commissions of inquiry are appointed and in certain cases, criminal cases are registered against police officers who used or said to have used *excessive* force. Indian Police Act - 1861 which was enacted by the British did not envisage accountability for the police. The British who wanted the police to use force against the then agitated Indian masses did encourage the police to be aggressively violent against the people. Democracy does not favour it and the result is that the police can not become aggressively cruel to people in a democracy. Still, the Indian Police Act - 1861 is in force and the policemen hold the view that they can afford to be aggressive to suppress any law and order disturbance in society. I believe that this is a wrong interpretation of the statute and therefore, it becomes necessary to tell the police that they have limitations when they involve themselves in law and order management in a democratic setup.

In a democracy, the people are more powerful than the police and the police can do nothing without public participation. The ruling government which has an eye on the vote bank may not like to displease the people and therefore the government may not favour anything which the people in their organized capacity and political strength may do. In certain instances police officers become casualties and precisely therefore, the police functionaries have to take maximum caution when they resort to strategies to deal with people who cause law and order disturbance in society.

Students are a powerful bloc and often they are patronized by political parties. Politicians sponsored students' organizations do manythings causing serious law and order disturbance and violence in society. Some of the earlier student-leaders have become State/National level politicians and many of them have come up by creating law and order disturbance in society. Police entry to educational institutions and their handling of student-unrest by iron hands are unfavourably viewed by the press, media and politicians. Police who are legally bound to maintain law and order come between devil and deep sea when they handle student agitations. They may lose the support of students and politicians and in such a situation, police become helpless. If they do not take action and deal with the situation, they may have to face departmental actions and will be made a target of adverse criticism by the media, press and a section of the society. On the contrary, if they manage the situation by resorting to lathies, rifles and tear gas shells, they are attacked mercilessly criticising that they use excessive force on student community. Many a time, the police do not have a proper scale in their hand to decide the quantity of force to be employed to establish law and order. The policemen become at their wit's end in many such situations.

A number of criminal cases may be registered in connection with any law and order disturbance. Nevertheless, when the disturbance comes to an end, probably all the cases registered will be withdrawn and resultantly, the police become a laughing stock. I do not understand the meaning of this sort of exercise and the police who claim to enjoy power and authority is converted into *nobody* who watches the rituals and ritualistic performances helplessly. What is more? If at all, in some cases, the criminal cases are not withdrawn, then the police lose their interest in the further progress of the case. For they know that they may not find out proper witnesses to prove the cases or if at all they are able to find out witnesses, they are likely to become hostile to prosecution when the cases come for trial. This procedure, I may look at it, is nothing but a mockery of justice administration.

Governments come and governments go and accordingly, the cases registered in connection with law and order disturbances also come and go. Even more harmful than the withdrawal of cases is the vindictive reactions to police officers who manage a law and order situation when a different political party is in power. What can or what should police officers do then remains undecided during law and order management.

Management is a nice term and many do not know what it means exactly. Does it mean '*avoid responsibility*'? Does it mean '*become active*' keeping maximum restraint? Does it mean '*do everything*' even by using force to suppress the violence? In any case, doubts remain as they are, although the lathy drill and mob operations taught in police training institutions remain to be as they were in the preindependent period. The jabs and cuts still rule the lathy drill although the concepts of using minimum force at a scene of law and order violence have considerably changed after India became independent.

Labour disputes and consequent law and order violence may be seen everywhere in the Country. Political attitude is that the police must, as far as possible, keep away from the labour sites where negotiation, persuation, conciliation etc., may work better. However, the police presence may be required to cause a certain amount of fear and terror in the locality. The employers and the employees may fight against each other to come to a compromise and work together for mutual benefits. The strikes, *dharnas*, processions and street corner meetings organized by the labourers are taken in a sportsman spirit and often, they become transitory/transient phenomenon. They cause law and order disturbance and mass scale destruction to public/employers' property and the police, as usual, register criminal cases to be withdrawn subsequently when the disputes are settled. What is more? The police here becomes again an agency of people's mockery and the police actions become just ritualistic exercises which are done as routine procedures in labour disturbances.

I have my own doubts. I used to ask: "What exactly fall under *law and order crimes?"* What is really meant by law and order? If a road procession is conducted causing serious disruption for free vehicular movements, it is not called law and order disturbance. It is known as a *procession on roads* and the police functions mean just escorting the procession so that the participants do not cause destruction to property belonging to others. The policemen are taught something about crowd control, mob operation, understanding crowd, mob and group etc., and most of them are confused about what to do and how to go about when they deal with law and order situations. A head constable who shot at people on a *bandh* day was judicially punished subsequently. People and public interest organizations raised their voice against the police so much so that the police became helpless to fight back the people, politicians and the press. Police may be powerful under law but is powerless before the people and the press/media. In a democracy, politicians dictate many things to police and the police, sometimes, become vulnerable to politicians' wishes and whims. Police are public servants and precisely therefore, the police can not do anything without taking into account the public sentiments and reactions to what they do during a law and order management. There was a time the police could do many things secretly, but today, they have to be transparent. Everything the police do at the site of a law and order management is videographed by many – is photographed by still more and may be publically exhibited. The police now can not say "this and that" after a mob operation as the people have the videotapes of everything that takes place at the scene. The press may bring out truth, half truth and falsehood. They give the news so much so that the people who read the news, often, become hostile to police. The general public have a tendency to support the people more than what they do with the police. The press/media may cash on public interest on people's causes and sell their commodity. The police become a casuality in such situations. The police versions have no survival value in such situations!

Who is Interested in Police ?

A question is often asked: “who is interested in police in a democracy?”. The interest of the people on an organization depends considerably on the nature of the output the organization ensures to people. People are interested in educational institutions, for they can get their children educated. They are interested in hospitals, for they can get their diseases treated. What is the interest the people have on police? The police can register criminal cases, but the people see that a majority of criminal cases registered go undetected and unpunished. People understand that the preventive role of the police in the commission of crimes is lesser than what was thought earlier. People see crimes being committed in front of and in spite of police. They also understand that the police are not able to prevent many crimes which affect the society very badly. They prevent crimes of petty nature having law and order dimensions temporarily in a transient way. A whole chapter in this book is devoted for discussing the preventive role of police.

As the output of police is far away from being satisfactory, the people are disinclined to take interest/sustained interest on police. As such, today, many functions which have been traditionally done by organized police are being done by the people themselves. The prevention role, the detection role, the investigation role, the traffic control role, the safety and security role and the law and order role of police are being taken up by the people in very many ways. I know that certain establishments maintain their own private 'Police system' to keep law and order in their organizations. Some resort to “goondas “and hired gangs” for the purpose. During a bus strike, the bus owners appointed their own people (goondas) to maintain their property. According to them, maintaining their own “Police force” may be cheaper than depending on the organized police service. Police conduct patrolling to prevent crimes and people appoint their own security personnel to guard their property. People today understand that the in-put to retain the police service is very heavy and the out-put is far away from being satisfactory. Why? Politicians and people themselves may be responsible to make the police inactive, inefficient or inoperative. Whatever that be, a tree is judged from the fruits it bears and likewise, an organization is evaluated from the service it renders to the society and people. Indian Police Act-1861 did not envisage all these social and political changes when it was drafted about one and half a century ago. The museum piece legislation can not make the police efficient or effective in the changing or already changed socio-political scenario. The law and order crimes of the pre-independent India are not the law and order crimes of today. This is a time one may see government sponsored *bandhs* during which the ruling political party itself may instigate people to violate laws and the police to watch them helplessly. In other words, in such circumstances, the law and order disturbance may be police sponsored(?) How can the sponsoring agency initiate steps to control law and order violations then? The police may do "this and that" to convince the people that they are doing a lot of things to manage the law and order situations! The police are neither able to convince the people nor control the law and order disturbance in such situations. People lose their trust and confidence in police activities and they try to see the police in bad shape. Police adopt many tactics and they are viewed with suspicion and their effectiveness seen with serious doubts. Delayed arrival at the scene of law and order disturbance, delayed decision - making there, escape mechnisms and shutting the eye tactics at the site, refusal to give orders etc.. are disfavoured.

Law and order disturbance is seen, frequently, in urban areas or at places where there can be scope for the same (for example, at a factory site). However, the government sponsored law and order disturbance may be seen everywhere. Recently, the political parties ruling the government declared a State-wide *bandh* and ruling government made police arrangements to tackle the situation. This may be called hypocrisy in a democracy and the people are yet to understand the hollowness in such political and police strategies to fool the people. People who promote law and order disturbance today become rulers tomorrow and they may try to justify their acts earlier. They may criticize the opposition for the law and order violations they cause at present. In street corner meetings and leaf-lets, people see attacks and counter-attacks by political parties and the police are dragged into the scene. The credibility of police as a law and order machinery becomes at stake and the people can not be convinced about police impartiality then at the appropriate time.

Many police officers have told me that they were good law and order managers. What did they mean by that? They meant that they could go in a police vehicle in their jurisdiction and cause fear and terror among people that they were at work. The same police officers have further told me that they were not good in crime investigation and scriptory works. I have felt that their notion and concept about law and order management were faulty and did not correspond to what was envisaged under the Indian Police Act - 1861. Patrolling a jurisdiction is not meant for law and order management. It is considered as a strategy for assuring the people of the police presence in the jurisdiction. The effect of patrolling for prevention of crimes on a more or less permanent basis is at best suspicious. The presumption is that the more is the police patrolling, the less will be the commission of crimes. But, experience shows that the more is the police patrolling, the more will be the precautions taken by criminals to commit crimes. The visible presence of police in particular area may advert the crime-doers to other areas where the visibility of police presence is minimum.

Police have elaborate arrangements to collect intelligence with regard to law and order disturbance. Such arrangements may help the police to take preventive and precautionary steps to control law and order disturbance. Nevertheless, they will be temporary as the police are not able to do much to eradicate the root causes of such law and order disturbance. Any steps taken by police will be at the surface level. The source level causes remain there as they are. Terrorism, naxalism, bomb blast etc.. are seen in society as the administration fails to tackle the causes of such convictional crimes at the source. Some of the law and order crimes have their roots at the socio-economic and political conditions prevailing in the country. Unless and until such sources are attacked, any surface management of law and order by police remain only at the peripheral levels. That is the reason why convictional criminals continue to operate here and there in spite of police vigil.

Criminalization of politics and politicization of criminals work as very powerful sources of law and order crimes. The trend is to show leniency to criminals when politicians commit crimes. The crimes committed by politicians, as I said earlier, are called political crimes and this is a wrong concept. Politicians make use of their political power and contacts to escape law enforcement. The impact is that politicians' crimes are treated as political crimes and this sort of treatment is a cause of law and order crimes. This is called politicisation of criminals and thus they get a political status even for the crimes they commit. Police become helpless and inactive in such circumstances. Then, they become quite incapable of preventing such crimes.

People who have criminal records enter politics to get a political coverage for the crimes they commit. Some politicians are accused of involving themselves in the commission of many traditional crimes and they face trials before the courts of law. Owing to their political affiliations, they walk as heroes and act as heroes and thus their criminal personality is white-washed by their political linkages. The politicians–businessmen - bureaucrats nexus make them to involve in the commission of crimes with adequate financial and bureaucratic patronage and support. Their activities which are criminal in nature get undue publicity in the media so much so that the crimes they commit are glorified. The police are forced to accommodate with such glorifications of crimes and criminal activities. The effect is that the law and order situations get worsened and the police become inactive as they are severely handicapped to initiate criminal proceedings against these powerful lobbies in politics, business and bureaucracy. Indian Police Act - 1861 did not think of these sorts of law and order issues and precisely therefore did not confer any special authority to police to deal with situations of like nature.

Violence and Law and Order

Violence has got connection with the law and order position of the society. Police come as agents to control violence and they feel it to be their duty to do so. If necessary, the police are empowered by law to have recourse to the use of violence. Police here want to maintain the '*Status quo*' and to reestablish harmony. Police make use of repressive tactics to deal with violence and they have noble purpose–i.e., establishing law and order. In earlier years, the police could use force without an accountability, but today they are made accountable. Politicians cash on the dead/ injured to their advantage and convert them to votes. If three or four firings by police result in the death of a few persons and a few lathi charges here and there by the police will make any ruling government to many problems to the extent of collapse. Police can not use force as often as they want and as powerful as they want. They are expected to use only minimum force at reducible minimum occasions. Any excessive force used by police will be termed as police atrocities and the government in power will have to face the consequences. Police are not considered as government servants. They are public servants and therefore, their accountability is more to the public than to the government in power.

People evaluate police actions and pass judgements on the basis of the public morality. The press and media evaluate the same, the police and the government do the samething and thus a public opinion is formed on the use of force by police. The opinion may be "necessary, sufficient, minimum, excessive etc." and thus the police earn good or bad name. Any action by police to reestablish the disturbed law and order may be short lived and as such the police action is only a relief and not a remedy at all for any sort of violence in society.

Law and order management by force is the last resort in a democracy. The people on the other side are Indians – the brothers, sisters, friends, kith and kin and so on. Hence, repressing the violence by violence is not considered to be the successful police action and therefore it must be resorted only in the rarest of rare occasions. Use of paramilitary forces or army men may not be favoured by the citizenry in a democracy. Terrorism, insurgency, naxalism etc.. are considered on different footing and such anti-government activities are repressed by force. Even while the police do so, they are expected to respect the human rights of the people. Once anyone is taken into custody by the police, he deserves to be treated as a person enjoying human rights! The complaint from the police is that the people attack them by weapons or stone them without any provocation. In spite of protective devices used by the police, several policemen are injured when they manage law and order situations. This is a serious problem which the citizenry must take note of and they need to be educated about citizens' responsibility in a demoracy. Political parties must take the initiative. Instead, they are blamed to instigate their followers to attack the police who wear the uniform to maintain them and to protect the people who have reposed confidence on police. Unscrupulous politicians cash on public agitations and police reactions to such agitations. Fishing in disturbed waters must not be the policy of any political parties. Policemen are their brothers, friends, kith and kin and they extend their services to people who are helpless and handicapped. This idea must go into the people and the media/ press can inculcate this into the people. Some press/media make attempts to project the police always in bad shape and this media approach causes more harm than good to the police personnel and to the administration. When the police are harmed unjustifiably, they harm themselves and the society.

Violence is no solution to any problems although it may speed up decision making. Administration must accept this fact. There was a time the police thought that muscle power was more important than mind power. Yes, it was so and the police could cause terror and fear among the public. The people literally feared the police. Gradually, money power exerted influence upon politicians and police and thus a situation emerged that money power became more important than muscle power and later the *mind power* became more important than money power and muscle power in a democracy. Law and order management by *mind power*-intelligently-with the aid of muscle power and money power becomes the style today. And I think that the style will pay rich dividends in the years to come. Muscle power of police has found to be ineffective during the investigation of crime and likewise, the muscle power is counter-productive in police administration. A police service which causes terror and fear or which threatens people might be a nineteenth century concept. Owing to the development of democratic values and democratic rule the police want to be more people friendly than to be power-mongering and authoritative. Police—a friend in need; a friend indeed may be what the people want now. In such a changed environment, law and order management through people's participation may be the only option left with the police. Like prevention of crimes, law and order management also must be a joint enterprise of police and the people.

Police Skepticism

Many police officers are skeptic of the success of police administration through people's participation. I do not know why they think in this way? If people can elect a government, rule the people in a democracy, maintain a police system etc.., why cann't they participate in police administration by extending their support and co-operation in prevention of crime, law and order management, in crime investigation? For this, the police must open the doors and permit the people to come in. Police must become more transparent and should welcome the people to come closer to them. Police ego may be a barrier for many people to come closer to police and it is time that the police realize the fact that police ego still comes out of a perverted notion about police role and functions in a democracy. People are the patrons and their support and participation become a *canditio sine qua non* for the success of police mission during the millennium. Skepticism has no scope here when realities show otherwise. Police today enjoy only those limited authority conferred upon them by the people. The people can take away the authority if they want. It being so, it is a wonderful idea that the policing is done with the aid and participation of the people in the democracy.

5

Police - People Relation: What is it ?

Police - people relation: What is it? I have asked this question several times to me and to others. Every time, I get different-different answers and even now I do not know what exactly is this police - people relation!

I saw three men in a police station. I asked each one of them: "How do you come to police station?".

One answered me: "I am caught and brought by the police on patrol duty".

The second one: "I come to police station as a petitioner".

The third one: "I am called by the police to become a witness".

I did not ask them to tell the nature of relationship they had with the policemen. For I could more or less guess it. I had seen during nineteen hundred and seventees in Sagar, Madhya Pradesh, policemen taking several people chained together to police stations. There were no human rights activists then. Even in nineteen hundred and ninety when I went to Sagar once again, I could see the same sight. I never wanted to ask them: "What type of relationship you have with the police?". For, I knew what type of relationship they would have had with the policemen.

Policemen have relations with businessmen - with politicians- with the higher ups in society – with the affluent and the influential- with the criminals and underworld dadas – with women, children and ordinary men on the street - with suspects, complainants, witnesses and a variety of people in society. What type of relationship do the people have with the policemen? I think that there is relationship but it varies considerably with the type of people who have contacts with the policemen.

Policemen include all - from constables to the director general of police. All wear the uniform and all enjoy power and authority in varying degrees. Each one of them maintains contacts with people, but the nature of relationship varies depending upon the type of people the policemen contact.

Departmental and Extra-departmental Relations

Certain people want to establish relationship with police officers of all ranks. For, they can survive well only if they maintain good relationship with the police department in general and individual policemen in particular. Spurious liquor manufacturers make regular payments to many in the police hierarchy and the purpose is to keep them in good humour. They consider their payments as an investment to their business. Once, I asked an Abkari contractor: "What type of relationship you have with the police?". He honestly said: "We have good relationship and our relationship is for the survival and success of our liquor business". Yes, there is a point in what he said. Perhaps, all over the world, such type of business relationship exists between policemen and businessmen of vested interests.

I do not know how far he is right. A senior police officer (He is no more now) once told me: "I worked as a sub-inspector in a port town. One day, a smuggler came to me and said that I could drive a car from the port town to another town and leave a packet to a person named and then take the car for yourself".

The smuggler came for entering into a business contact and any sub-inspector who did not own a car might be tempted to drive the smuggled items to the destination and thus had a car. If he was unscrupulous, he might even enter into a regular business contract. The criminals and underworld dadas, smugglers and unprincipled men make attempts to establish relationship with the police, for they want to exploit the advantages and privileges of the uniform for their business profits. In films and T.V. serials, one could see such unholy relationship between police and criminal gangs. Some policemen work as members of the gang? The officer mentioned above retired rich and died rich and he had a rich cremation.

Relationship via weakness – this may be an area for research. Find out the weakness in a person and make attempts to compensate the weakness and that is the strategy some people adopt to establish relationship. Some police officers want position in life and certain posts to occupy. Politicians know it well and they see to it that such officers are picked up and posted. Thereafter, they start establishing relationship for their mutual advantage. The relationship is professional - political or vice versa and both stand to gain through such contacts and relationship.

Amidst temptations, it may be difficult for many to withstand them. Money, fortune, liquor, women, position, contact or anything can be tempting forces and some yield to temptations easily while some others take sometime to become victims of temptations. A corrupt man establishes relationship for corrupting the police and he may bring anything for this purpose. Even politicians of international stature become vulenerable to sexual temptations. If everything some police officers speak is true, then sex plays an important role in police interactions with certain categories of people. Sexual temptations are offered to unmarried officers - to middle aged - to officers who experience sexual starvation and to officers at the fag end of their career.

Corruption means many things and includes many things. "I could not make anything from my service and I am retiring within an year. I want a posting in the General Executive Branch"– requested to the deputy inspector general of police by a sub-inspector. The intentions were clear and they could be anything other than justice administration. Necessarily, he might establish his contacts with such people who would be able to help him to make something from his service. The deputy inspector general of police looked at him and gave a posting and said: "Let him make something. He has served the department so long but could not make anything".

What type of relationship do police officers/men maintain with people? This depends upon individual police officers and the nature of transactions they have with the people. The relationship can be official or non-official. Some studies show that non-official relationship is more and stronger than official relationship. Studies also show that people generally do not maintain good relationship with police officers for friendship alone. Many relationships have depths and widths more than what they appear to be at the surface level. I have noticed the people who used to come to the marriages of the sons/daughters of certain police officers and I could find people of all descriptions participating in the marriage-feasts, all claiming to be very close to the police officers who have invited them for the marriages. A police officer once said: "Study the telephone calls a police officer receives everyday and you can know the nature of relationship he has with people". Police officers receive greeting cards, marriage invitations, special invitations for dinner/lunch etc. and they show the type of people who associate with them. Police officers who want to have only official relations with people may feel isolated and unattended; but will be able to administer justice to people in a more honest and objective way. Such police officers may have only short survival value and may be evicted by forces which are beyond their control. I wrote this much just to show that police - people relationship has many dimensions which are not discussed by many.

Police are still viewed as a force (not service) by many. An association with police officers is still considered as a licence to do many things which they can not do otherwise. Some well to do people want to associate with police officers just to make others known of their contacts with police circles. Such people have a free entry to police stations without fear or apprehensions of *Police treatment* which is abhorred by many. Usually, ordinary people go to police stations with introductions and recommendations when these privileged groups can just walk into police stations!

Police officers know well that certain *designations* have more deterrent value among the public. An assistant commandant in an armed batallion is not feared as much as a deputy superintendent of police in the General Executive Branch. Hence, some assistant commandants always like to be known as deputy superintendent of police in public. The same attitude is seen among some of the armed police inspectors, armed police sub - inspectors and so on. It being so, a relationship with the people by causing a certain amount of fear in them seems to dominate the police circles. This sort of *relationship by fear* is not natural and is seen more among the middle, lower middle and lower class people in society.

'Respect' shown to people out of fear/apprehension of something bad may fall on them is not respect. It may be a psychological game played and therefore it is often called hypocrisy in people-police relationship. *Parade-ground* discipline inculcated to police personnel makes some to be hypocritical in their inter-personnel relations. Here one sees a superior with authority and an inferior without any authority. Fear and anxiety work between them and the impact is an artificial type of respectful relationship between the two-the lower taking a submissive attitude while the higher showing an authoritarian attitude. A similar relationship is found operative in interactions between police officers and people in the lower or lowest strata of the society.

'Police are grass for us' - a slogan in vernacular is often heard when people organize jathas and anti-government demonstrations. This slogan is often heard more loudly when the people know that the police are likely to repress the people's demonstration. Why do the people shout slogans in that way? – I used to think and ask the question directly to the demonstrators.

I think that they tell alike. The slogan signifies that the police are not grass and people can not trample over them. They are literally afraid of police and the slogan is only an outward expression of the inside fear in people. Can the police establish a sort of smooth and healthy relationship with people who are fearful of the police? I do not think that it is easily possible. Hence, they may try to avoid the police wherever possible and whenever necessary.

In cities, I have seen the residences of many senior officers and middle/upper middle level officers. They have police sentries at home and the people generally keep a safe distance from many of them. They do not want to associate with police officers who possess pistols, canes, batons and security guards. I have asked many residents in the locality where senior police officers reside and quite a few of them told me that they would prefer to keep a safe distance as they are afraid of them. Many senior level officers are nice people; but are not viewed so and the prime reason is the fear people have for them. People look at them from a distance and see them as people possessing an authoritarian ego with assumed seriousness on their faces. They do not see human faces in many? The impact is avoidance at any cost. How can the police establish good human relations with people if they are not prepared to come closer to police or the police not prepared to go closer to people?. If avoidance is seen in residential areas, it will be more in official transactions.

Police are given official vehicles to perform their duties. They are fitted with special lights and have inscription as police. In cities, one may notice that these police vehicles moving in high speed without giving due regard to other fellow passengers. Police vehicles are considered as a licence to commit certain traffic violations and the people who see them develop an unfavourable disposition towards such traffic violators. People assess the need and necessity for the police to behave the way they do and when they find that the misbehaviour is only a projection of an authoritarian ego or projection of pseudo - authority, they are disinclined to appreciate the police behaviour. They murmur and mumble against the police. Police officers who have no authority to control traffic too play with their vehicles causing displeasure in public. Once a police driver disobeyed the signal shown by a traffic constable. The inspector general of police later suspended him from service. His callous indifference to traffic signals was not to be viewed lightly as it could cause a traffic accident on the road. People do not react openly or resent against the police violations of traffic laws, because they are afraid of raising their voice against the police. They repress their emotions which may be expressed in their later interactions with the police. Can the police establish an enviable relationship with people when they are not prepared to respect human dignity of fellow passengers on road?.

There are any number of V.I.Ps now and some of them have police pilots/escorts. The way, the pilot vehicles are running on the roads and the way the policemen seated in the pilot vehicle behave cause, at times, irritation among the people. The words uttered by the policemen escorting the V.I.P. may not be palatable to a decent man on the street. The impact is that people helplessly consume the escort or pilot behaviour. They express their reactions through cultural media and the people who enjoy the programme endorse the negative reactions to police behaviour.

Generally, the people are not in favour of escorts and pilots for some *ineligible* V.I.Ps. Many a time, the reactions of people towards so many escorts and pilots have appeared in the press. They talk about it often and in such an atmosphere of negative public feelings, the policeman's enthusiastic behaviour is likely to cause further irritation among the people. There was a Chief Minister in a aparticular State. He used to travel in overspeed with escorts/pilot vehicles. Once he was defeated in a poll and many people then commented: "The Chief Minister is defeated because people do not like the way he travels on roads". True or false the cause behind his defeat, the people were showing an irritative attitude to what the Chief Minister was showing while he was in power.

Can good police-people relationship develop in atmosphere which is pregnant with negative attitudes or irritating dispositions? I think that it difficult to have good human relations between the police and people in the existing situation. Why think in this way? People were, once, waiting in a queue to purchase railway tickets. Two policemen came in uniform and without showing any consideration to the people waiting in the queue went to the ticket counter and got the tickets issued. People in the queue commented: "Look at these policemen. They have no laws to abide by". I do not think that it was a laudable comment that can be made on public servants whose duty it is to be models for others. At least, they purchased tickets, But, allegations are often heard that many policemen do not purchase tickets when they travel in private transport omnilus. Why? They have given an impression to the vehicle owners that it would be better if the policemen were given free travel in their transport vehciles. Some middle level functionaries travel in taxi-cabs without paying the fare or sufficient fare. Some utilize privately owned vehicles-free of charges and they claim tthat they give a lot of concessions to such vehicle owners or they have "*good*" friendship with them. Whatever that be, the police-people relationship can be evaluated only in the background of what the police do and how the people view what the police do in society.

Police - People Relations in Work Related Areas

Elsewhere in this book, I have written that police work can become successful only if they get public participation. This new approach calls for more and more human relations between the police and the people. Will this be attainable?

In the background of many criminal cases being acquitted, it becomes necessary that there must be more and more public co-operation for the successful conduct of criminal cases. Defects in witness-testimony is the single most important factor for the large-scale acquittals. Police, it seems to me, have to recognize the fact that they can not become successful if they keep the witnesses at a distance as they do now. The witnesses evaluate the pros and cons of becoming witnesses in criminal cases. They weigh the advantages and disadvantages in giving testimony before police and the courts of law. There are very powerful forces working to win over prosecution witnesses and the police do not have a greater force to keep them on the side of the prosecution. The only thing the police possess may be their good will and human qualities.

There was a time the people were very much afraid of police and the ill-consequences if they showed negative attitudes to police cases. Now, the situation has changed so much so that the people don't care what may come if they speak this way or that way before the courts of law. In the absence of the inability of police to prove a crime by the help of scientific evidence and independent witness-testimonies, the police have no option other than relying on the available witnesses and that can be achieved only by ensuring the good-will of the witnesses at hand.

Witnesses are part of the society and they too entertain an avoiding attitude to police and cases investigated by police.A good number of them do not want to involve themselves in police investigation and prolonged court trials. Some of them do not find any meaning in seeing that the accused is punished after a long time since the commission of crimes. When a crime is committed, people have a retributive approach to the crime-doers. As time gets elapsed, the retributive attitude is lessened and lessened to the extent of becoming an attitude of sympathy, consideration and concern for the crime-doers. To some, criminal justice administration appears to be meaningless exercise intended for causing harassment to them and to the accused!

It is virtually very difficult for the police to maintain the good relations which they initially established with the witnesses. What is more? Many police officers come to the scene and the investigator who originally investigate the case goes to oblivion - never to be contacted and heard. The ties which the witnesses do establish with the original investigator too gets broken so much so that he loses his interest in the case. Police - informer relations, police - witnesses relations, police - victim relations thus turn out to be no relation at all. Police, in the meantime, get a number of new cases and to keep the witnesses, in old cases, close to them becomes a herculian task and practically an impossible task. When the press reports the judgements of an old case, the people try to refresh their old memories and say "all ends well that ends well".

Unless they have some vested interests, generally people do not want to establish any sort of relationship with police, doctors, courts and lawyers. It being the case, it is not right to think that the police can or should establish good relations with people for the purpose of making them witnesses in criminal cases. If the general behaviour of the police is nice and praiseworthy, then the people come closer and closer to the extent of becoming witnesses in criminal cases. Earlier, it has been brought out that the general police behaviour is far away from being satisfactory and precisely therefore to bring people as witnesses in police cases too is very difficult, if not impossible. Any human relation built up for a particular purpose-on a temporary basis-will not last longer. Police-witness relationship is of similar nature and therefore it may not be smooth if at all police want to be nice to them. If the police do not change their general behavioural patterns and tactics, then any attempt to establish a sort pasted relationship with witness will not yield good results. It will be an exercise in futility and a waste of time.

What type of relationship can the police establish with suspects in crimes? Some police investigators complain that the "suspect is not co-operating with the investigation". What do they mean by that? Do they mean that the suspect must extent his full co-operation to see that he goes to jail? Do they mean that together they can send the suspects behind bars? Necessarily, the police-suspect relationship will be hostile or enimical to each other. Use of third degree methods, coercion, concoction of evidence further worsen the relationship not only between the police and the suspect under interrogation, but also between the people in society and the investigators in the uniformed service. People in general are suspicious of police strategies during an investigation and they are inclined to think that the police resort to any fair and foul means against the suspects to prove a crime against them. In the prevailing circumstances, it may not be that easy to establish good human relationship with the people unless the police give an assurance to people that everything during an investigation will be done scientifically and psychologically. I have my serious doubts about the competance of many police investigators to do the job scientifically and psychologically. The people too entertain such impressions about the competance of police investigators. A police officer who is trained to do every type of job - from escort to anti - insurgency operations can be only a generalist in police work. What is needed is the service of specialists in investigation and interrogation. So long as it is not done, one wonders whether or not the police can earn the required rapport from the general public. People keep away from police because of their lack of confidence in the police specialization in the area of work. Police conception of success in investigation is socially unacceptable, for, the people still think that crimes are not investigated in the proper way. Instances are not rare that innocent people are chargesheeted by police after a fair investigation as they claim it to be. It would seem, then, that two human emotions are strongly working in public minds against police investigation and they are fear and hatred. The purpose of investigation is to prove the truth and certainly, it must give an air of respectability for the investigating machinery. But, when the people see that the investigating exercise offers or multiplies only human misery, then they think several times whether or not they must co-operate with police to cause further misery.

Prevention of crime is an impossible task in any society and police alone can do the least towards that end unless they get public participation. Most people have in the background of their minds a haunting fear of crimes and this is especially true of people who have wealth and property. The rich fear of burglary, theft, robbery etc. and the poor fear of their safety and security. Both are engaged in the protection of their life and property and they want to achieve it by the help of police. Hence it must be one of the priority concerns of police to co-operate with people in their endeavour to prevent crimes in society. I doubt very much whether or not the police have accepted this reality! If at all they have accepted it, I do not think that they are designing and devising strategies to get maximum public co-operation and participation in their crime - prevention campaigns. The police are still conscious of IPC crimes, but the people are terror-striken owing to new forms of crimes that are not seen on the pages of the Indian Penal Code-1860. Many IPC crimes are just the by-products of new crimes and any attempt to prevent IPC crimes can not stop the emergence of new crimes unless the police try to get public participation in the prevention of new crimes. Some of the new types of crimes are discussed elsewhere in this book.

Public are aware of the new types of crimes and the media brings them out occasionally. The cultural media shows them in theatres and elaborates them in novels etc. Yet, the public do not come forward to combat the emerging profile of new crimes, because they do not get adequate support from agencies responsible for preventing crimes in society. Healthy police - people interaction can help a lot to prevent crimes, but it seems that there exists only little or very little relation between the police and the people.

People may come to police with a request to register a F.I.R and if the police refuse to do so in spite of clear provisions under the Code of Criminal Procedure - 1973, it is nothing but non-co-operation with people in their attempt to prevent crimes. Sometimes, anonymous letters may be sent to police on commission of crimes. The police can ignore them. Also they can initiate actions to prevent the commission of crimes. If the people are given an assurance that anonymous letters will be taken in due seriousness, then they may come forward in large numbers in the prevention activities of police. Telephone calls and press-reportings of crimes may be another source of information for the police to act upon. People require an assurance of safety and security if they must volunteer information on crimes and support the police in their mission.

This is a time of Panchayat Raj and certainly, crime prevention is possible through them. But, they must be educated to do what is required. A lot of voluntary organizations committed for social welfare are at work. School teachers can be used as an effective tool to educate children to fight against crimes. Religious agencies can be profitably made use of for the purpose. For all these, the police must go to them rather than waiting for the people to come to police for preventing crimes in society. No crime can be prevented eternally, yet, timely action taken by police can stop temporarily atleast the commission of crimes. Constant and continuous vigil by the people and the police may be very effective to prevent crimes for a longer period. Concurrently, society building agencies can be utilized to make long term planning to curb down the extent of criminal behaviour in a particular locality. Experience shows that police work with society builders has brought out enviable out put in the prevention of crimes. Association with such agencies may open new vistas for better police people relationship.

Somehow or other, an impression has gone deep into the minds of people that police want to establish relations with the people only to make them witnesses in police cases. The impression has to be changed and for that purpose, the police must come forward with new strategies and action plans to enlist more and more public participation in other areas of police work. "United we stand, divided we fall" must be the police idea for the millennium. No police without people and no people without police- let it go deep into police minds and let it work strongly in the years to come.

Police Aid Posts established in bus stations and railway platforms can be an effective source to strengthen police-people relationship. "Our caution; your safety"– this motto was exhibited in front of an exhibition stall by police. The police pictured the idea by showing a hen protecting its chickens from the attack of a vulcher flying in the sky. It was well appreciated by the people who made a comment "only if the police are serious of what they show". Even there, one sees a lack of trust among people on police promises. It must therefore be the attempt of police to "walk to talk" of what they show as advertisement. On the side of the patrol cars, the police write: "To protect and serve". Really a marvellous idea if they can "walk to talk".

I do not know why the police in India did not allow the people to participate in crime prevention. In some foreign countries, members of the public are encouraged to go with the patrolmen on duty. This enables them to know how important is the patrol duty. They encourage members of the voluntary agencies to conduct independent patrolling and request them to get in touch with the police in case they want police services. The residents' associations in cities are taught to guard their areas and settle issues among them without police help. At a time when out of court settlement of cases are promoted, why not the people be encouraged to self-police the area where they reside. The primary duty of guarding self and property rests with individual citizens and the police have only secondary importance in such responsibilities which are incumbent on individuals. Self protection is the best precaution against crimes.

Maintaining good human relations with people was not given due importance in the past. By the time the need was badly felt, the people had travelled a long way from the police. In order to bring the people closer to police, a change in the sub-culture of police became necessary. The change was not easily attainable. To convince the police themselves about the need to work in close quarters with the people itself became a herculian task. Some half-hearted attempts were made here and there, but they did not yield the expected results. Development of a new attitude, outlook and approach among the policemen became inevitable. "Reorientation courses were organized in police training institutions. The police could realize that the people would not come to police and therefore the only option left has been to go to the people. Community policing and similar experiments have been conducted and the result is found to be quite encouraging. "People are the police and the Police are the people" – this idea already implemented by the British in their country long back got acceptance in India too recently. Having a lot of people, most of them living psychologically at a distance from the police, is no doubt an unpleasant thing in a democratic setup. People who lived very near to a police station too kept away from police and the reasons were obvious. I asked some to tell me why they kept away from police. About ten years ago, they said the cries they heard from the police compound were horrible and could cause mental agony in many of them. The same people tell me now that the situation has changed a lot after the enactment of the Protection of Human Rights Act-1993. How did the change come into being suddenly? The reason was that the police were made accountable for what they did after 1993. Police activities are being watched minutely and are appropriately dealt with. Police become fearful of the people particularly the human rights activists. People's fear of police is getting diminished and the police are forced to become people friendly-human rights friendly in their activities. The change is certainly a welcome one and it takes the police in the right direction to the third millennium. The police understand now that when they deny or neglect their fundamental relationship to the people, they think that they are their own rule and measure. This attitude can not do any good or work any longer.

Police - People Relationship: A Myth or Reality?

Police must exist and people must exist and there should be some relationship between the two. One is a control mechanism and the other is the controlled. The relationship is that of a controller and the controlled. Can it be like the parents and children? I do not think it to be so. For, the parents not only control their children, but also look after the physical, personal, educational, psychological and personality development needs. The relationship is stronger and there is a mutual recognition. Can it be like the teachers and pupils? No. I can not agree with a proposition that the police - people relationship is like teachers and students. The functions of teachers are education and human formation. Then, can it be like religion and its followers? Yes, to some extent, for, religious authorities and the followers have a common objective. Probably, the police and the people have a common objective .i.e, harmonious living and social welfare. Do the police perform their functions adequately? I have my own doubts. For, allegations are heard that the police are not just. They are blamed to torture the people, use third degree methods, employ their muscle power excessively, concoct evidence in criminal cases, adopt fair and foul means to administer justice and as such people think that an instrument created to ensure human happiness turns out to be at times an instrument to cause human misery. The purpose for which police service is maintained is not actualized. Or, if at all the police try to do so, the people are not convinced about it. There is lack of trust and consequently, the relationship between the police and the people becomes strange and far away from being satisfactory. This is a dilemma that we face today.

The police is a mass and the people too are a mass. There are individuals in the mass and the relationship is between individuals. If relationship between the two must be good and for that the human contacts between the individual member of the public must be fine. All values in human contacts must be meticulously observed. There must not be ego - conflicts. Man and policeman are human beings – social beings – beings whose relationship is guided by human values. To exist, for man and policeman, is to coexist. To be in police means to be with other people in society. It is in this connection only one may think of police - people relationship. Police must be open and their openness to people make the relationship possible and laudable. Except a few anarchists, everyone wants healthy police-people relationship. But, there exists some crediblity crisis.

relationship. But, there exists some crediblity crisis. People have lost their trust on police. The lost trust must be regained and then only good relationship can be established.

Human rights friendly approach by police to people can certainly improve the relationship. People friendly police may be an old concept, but is an imporant concept in a democracy. Human rights of all people must be respected and must not be marked by surprising contradictions in police work. The very rights for life, liberty, equality and dignity are solemnly proclaimed and publicly affirmed in India. If the police deny them to the citizenry or trample upon item, then how can the people come closer to police? There must be a proper sensitivity in acknowledging the value and dignity of every individual as a human person with dignity. Can the police repudiate the provisions of human rights law in practice? Experience shows that they do. The people know that the primary objective of the police service today is the protection of human rights of people. Do the police recognize it? Perhaps, the archaic Indian Police Act-1861 does not speak of it. Some of the police acts geopardize the very meaning of democratic coexistence. In such a situation, how can the police-people relationship be improved? For it, the police must change their attitude and approaches to people. This change must come from within the police hearts. By their changed attitudes and approaches, they must effect a corresponding change among the people. The people must have trust on police and police sense of justice—just justice—equal justice—gender justice human rights justice, social justice and victim justice.

6

Police Ethics: What Does it Mean ?

Police ethics – there is nothing like that and this is said by a very senior police officer. I wrote a chapter on.police morality in my book "*Indian Police - 2001: What Went Wrong Here*?" Mr. Netto Desmond, and an inspector general of police in Kerala State once told me that the police ought to teach police morality compulsorily in police training institutions, for, he thought that the area was very much neglected. Perhaps, that was the main motive for me to include a full chapter on police morality in my earlier book and here.

Police ethics is still viewed by many, perhaps by most people, as something that does not exist. Can the police be ethical? people ask me this question when they know me as one teaching police officers. Power corrupts man and absolute power corrupts man absolutely–this is often heard and if that is true, power corrupts policeman. Can power be ethical?–can a policeman be ethical?

Some police officers say that police can just ignore ethics like that. They need to be only legal – i.e., act according to law and the procedure established by law. All legal things, they argue, are not ethical and all ethical things are not legal. I am not interested to create a controversy on the issue. Nevertheless, I can say emphatically that all legal things are not always ethical. Certain legal acts are unethical. Legal acts mean that the acts are accepted as lawful by the State's law for the time being. But ethical laws are eternal and are not limited to time and space. A few decades ago, a criminal had to immerse his palm into boiling oil to prove his innocence. If burnt, he did commit the offence, if not, he was innocent. It was perfectly legal to do so. But morally? The moralists argued: "The law enforcement agencies–the judge included-should first immerse their palms into the boiling oil and could see whether or not they got burnt. As they were not criminals, certainly, they ought not to burn". But, they did not do so, and the law prevailed in southern parts of South India. Again, a king cobra might be put into a large jar and the criminal had to put his hands into the jar. The law was that he would be presumed to be innocent if the snake did not bite him. If the snake attacked him by biting, then he was guilty. It was legal to do so. Nevertheless, what was the moral aspect? I must confess that both were unethical and therefore could not survive longer.

Society is changing and correspondingly the social outlook gets changed. Conditions in the present world are working to effect a change in public attitude towards police and police attitude towards the public. Police once thought that it was legitimate for them to administer *instant justic*e to petitioners who came to police stations with issues relating to civil matters. They could not be blamed for what they did. For, *instant justice* was a concept developed by police for finding out easy and speedy solutions to people's problems. I am told that in some North Indian States, in earlier days, the officer in charge of police stations went to distant villages to dispose of petitions instantly by calling petitioners and counter petitioners. Making a visit to the spot of dispute listen to the petitioners and counter petitioners and take a decision instantly and enforce it with police authority, pseudo – authority, assumed authority and the muscle power of police. Allegations were plenty to show that the instant justice thus administered was not just. Corruption, bad influence, political intervention, police susceptibility to the powerful in society affected adversely and destructively to some of the instant justices administered by police. Though people initially accepted police interference in petitions, they show reluctance to yield to police decisions now. After a perusal into the statutes governing police authority, people found out that the police were not authorized to administer instant justice especially in civil matters. Correspondingly, the public attitude changed and now it may be noticed that the police attitude to administer instant justice too gets changed. As far as human nature is concerned, it is just not possible for it to tolerate injustice even if it is supported by law. People resist and the result is a change in law. The change in law will have a stronger basis on the morality of the issue under discussion. The moral sense of the people guides the legal principles in any society. Morality comes from a social conscience wherein the guided principles are given more importance than the guiding principles.

Guiding Principles and Guided Principles

Police have many *guiding principles* which tell them what to do. All rules, regulations and police laws are the guiding principles. What is the ethics behind such guiding principles? Unless the policeman is made aware of the *guided principles* behind the guiding principles, they do not give due care to the morality of what they do. The *guided principles* speak of morality. If a policeman does everything as per the guiding principles, and he does not care for the guided principles, then his acts will not get public acceptance and approval. For, the society is concerned more with the guided principles and not with the guiding principles. This is the reason why moralists speak more about *norma normata* than about *norma normens.* I think that there is a lot of truth in what the moralists speak about. I am to think that the police must accept *norma normata* when they perform their duties. For example, there is a guiding principle, and it is: "No child shall he detained in police station": It is a law in the Juvenile Justice Act-1986 and a guiding principle for the police. What are the guided principles? The guided principles have come not one day, too soon. The guided principles are centuries old and they have basis on the moral, social and cultural conscience of people belonging to several centuries. The children were given special status and they were not treated on par with the adults. Consideration to the immaturity, age, intelligence, experience of children has been accepted all throughout the world – in all cultures and at all times. The police ought to recognize them when they enforce law. The guided principles have been well laid down in the United Nations' Standard Minimum Rules for the Administration of Juvenile Justice. Just see what the U.N speak about it. "Member States shall seek, in conformity with their respective general interests, to further the well being of the juvenile and her or his family". The U.N continue: "Member States shall endeavour to develop conditions that will ensure for the juvenile a meaningful life in the community, which during that period in life when she or he is most susceptible to deviant behaviour, will foster a process of personal development and education that is as free from crime and delinquency as possible". Accepting everything the U.N. tell about juvenile justice, the policemen ask: "why cann't a juvenile be kept in a police station? I know that the policemen who ask that question know the reasons behind and that is precisely the morality or ethics behind that guiding principle. Morality and ethics have their roots in the upright conscience of an individual. The guiding principles, as given in the juvenile Justice Act - 1986, define a juvenile as one below 16 years of age, if male and one below 18 years of age, if female. Knowing the guiding principles well, a police officer,after getting hold of male juvenile delinquent, wrote that he was 18 years of age and thus he wanted to overlook the provisions contained in the Juvenile Justice Act-1986. The behaviour of the police officer was against law and morality. It was a product of an *elastic conscience* and not of an *upright conscience*. The influence and impact of an *elastic conscience* make police acts, often, immoral and unpopular.

Pull Principles and Push Principles

The police are statutorily empowered to do certain acts and they have to do them, no matter they like to do them or not. The people will make them to do so, for, the people know that the police are meant for them. If a serious crime takes place, the police are forced to investigate it. There is not option other than investigating the case. The forces which pull a police officer to certain acts are called *Pull Factors* over which individual police officers have no control. I can not think – that the police do certain things as they are pulled by forces beyond their control that they are doing so because they are moved by morality or ethical principles. To a scene of crime, the police may come with dogs and dogmen and I know the intentions in conducting a 'dog - search' at the scene of crime. I have never treated such police behaviour as something moved by ethics and I do not feel that any sensible man may think that the *police show* at the scene of crime is a moral act.

More than the pull factors and principles, morality is based on the *Push Factors* which are coming from the "within" of the police officers. Duty consciousness, responsibility feelings, public expectations, social obligations, conscience prick and thus a number of forces operate as very powerful in a police officer and they together form the *Push Principles*. In fact, principles which are based on morality and good conscience make the police job noble and praise worthy. I, for one, am inclined to feel that today more emphasis is given to the pull principles than to the push principles and that is the reason why the police are afraid of criticisms and media. No doubt the push principles must be taught to police officers.

Like public tranquility, public order, public vision, public opinion, public attitude, public reaction etc. there is something called public morality or public ethics. People, invariably, evaluate police actions employing the public scales. If they find that the police ethics is contrary to public ethics, they react vehemently. As for example, the public honour gender dignity. If a woman is contacted by a police officer without showing due regard to her gender decency, the people react against it whatever may be the advantage the police make by enforcing law on her. People insist for a just justice system in which the woman should get due justice with strict regard to gender decency and gender dignity. When sex - workers – by proper name, the prostitutes – made complaints that some police officers were not gender decent to prostitutes, the public ethics was not in favour of police actions. People do not want to see police administering justice without being gender decent to male suspects and offenders in law. That is the reason, why police officers who keep the male detinues in half nakedness in police custodial facility is unfavourably viewed. The guiding principle may be to interrogate the suspects, but the guided principle is to do the same as per the ethical laws which guide the guiding principles. Human rights of people-detinues, offenders, victims of crime – must be fully respected.

In a democracy, the police are transparent and the people see and evaluate what the police do even inside the four walls of a police station. As the visibility of police actions become more and more conspicuous, the moral assessment of police actions will also be more and more easily done. People then say that the police may be right under the law to do things in the way they do, but are morally wrong. If that becomes the public assessment of what the police do legally, then the police cease to get public appreciation and approval of what the police do legally. Once, a police officer caught hold of an offender who confessed to the police that he committed the crime. Immediately, the police told him to make the confession before the court. He was given the assurance that the court would take a lenient view to the accused who made a clean confession. He was given a promise that he would be released free if he made a clean confession before the magistrate. Believing everything the police told him, he went to the court and confessed his crime. He was shocked to hear the judgement punishing him to imprisonment. He said later that he was cheated by the police. People who heard his narration said that the policemen committed wrong as he was given false promises. The people were prepared to forgive the offender for what he did, but were not prepared to forgive the police for what they did to a guilty accused. The police were badly criticised and then acts of the police caused public distrust on police promises. Public morality is very strong and goes against the police. The police are blamed to be "unethical" in their actions in such instances. Whatever may be the guiding principles for the police to behave the way they did, the guided principles were against the morality of a just justice system. Those police officers who commit an immoral act while they administer justice should recognize the fact that their immorality will not be tolerated even when they succeed in administering justice as per their definition of justice. Legally administered justice has – should have – moral content. Hence any justice administered without taking into account the moral contents can not become just justice to people.

False Notions about Police Ethics and Police Behaviour

Police believe that administration of justice promotes human happiness and social welfare. I agree with the argument, but I can not subscribe to the view that administration of justice is not what the police think about it. After an investigation of crime, the offender is punished and to that extent we many say that criminal justice is administered. But, for obtaining a conviction, suppose, the police concocted evidence and produced false witnesses etc. and I can not say that a conviction obtained by employing such obnoxious practices is administration of justice. The end may be praiseworthy, but the means adopted to reach the end must not be immoral. If illegal and immoral means and methods are taken to administer criminal justice, I can not say that the police succeed in administering just justice to the offender. Just justice contains moral elements more than anything else.

Moral principles are inculcated to a person from his childhood and the ethical values are thus indelibly written in his human conscience. One can not work in police keeping away his human conscience. The infantile personality pregnant with moral values work very powerfully even when one behaves as a police officer. There must not be a division between his police values and his infantile values. Some police officers argue that police values are different from infantile values and they do many things basing on their police values. But, I think that many police officers feel uneasy in heart when they do something (as a police officer) which goes against their infantile values. The mother, father, family, school, community, religion etc. inculcate human values which can not be easily wipped off even when one wears a police uniform. Crime is not an excusable act in any society, but the criminal, on account of that alone, should not be treated in an unjust way. In the process of criminal justice administration, the criminal is sometimes treated in a retributive spirit by the agencies empowered to deal with him in a human right friendly manner. This is the ethical law and therefore police officers must not commit immoral acts when they deal with crime-doers.

Is there a conflict between morality and justice in our police working? Police officers say that there exists a conflict between the two. How? For them, the moral conscience is different from legal conscience. They argue that one can be legal without being moral. The moralists ask a question: "Can we split conscience into many parts?". They feel that conscience is a whole that can not be cut into pieces according to one's subjective scales. What is moral will be legal and what is legal will be moral - or they ought to be like that. It is illegal to employ torture on a suspect. It is also immoral to use third degree methods on a suspect. Which moral law allows torture? It is immoral to call epithets on suspects. It is also illegal to do so. Which law of the State allows police to use filthy language? Hence, morality and legality are the two sides of the same. One can not exist without the other. To be legal means to be moral and to be moral means to be legal. If police must survive as a social institution then they must accept morality and legality as one and the same in police work.

Police Code of Ethics and Justice

A code of ethics for the police has been recognized now in India and I have discussed it in detail in my earlier books. Though the guiding principles in the Code are well written, many do not know the "guided principles" and therefore the Code remains as just a Code like that. Why did the Code come into existence? What were the circumstances which made the Code necessary? I am not interested to speak anything about them, nevertheless I can say that the emergence of a Code of ethics for police presupposes that the police have been behaving unethically. Police morality was not taken serious note of in police functionings. People felt the need for it and thus the Code was inacted.

Every law enacted has a human conscience behind it. Every law is the wish of the society. Every law has a spirit and every law has a purpose. Enforcement of law with a purpose and it is for the administration of just justice. My father told me once "law enforcement without a social commitment and accountability is no law enforcement". Then, he was talking about the ethics of law enforcement and that is what I wish every policeman – from the bottom constable to the top director general of police – must bear in mind when the law is enforced. Some constables have more ethical consciousness than some of the senior level functionaries and the reverse too is true. Hence morality is not the monopoly of certain ranks in police service. It is a value, a virtue, a quality and is there in every human conscience. The Code of Police Ethics may be taken only in that sense.

I wrote a book *Policing the Largest Democracy: 50 Years and After'* and I said emphatically that Indian police did a lot of enviable things in the past. But they failed to get adequate appreciation for what they did and one of the main reasons was that their behaviour was not beyond criticism and attack from the people. One doubts whether or not the police in India were morality conscious in their transactions. An ethics - friendly police service could only win the appreciation of people and that might be again one of the reasons for bringing out a special Police Code of Ethics at a later stage.

Police morality: What is it? It is not found in any statutes enacted by the British or later by Indian democracy. Ethics has been there is Indian Scriptures, literature, philosophy and social life and necessarily, it ought to be there in police service. But, some of the acts which the police did-torturing, harassing, humiliating etc. for examples-were not ethically accepted or pleasantly tolerated, but were helplessly suffered and silently reacted against. I am not making any attempt to give any analysis of the origin of the police morality as it exists today. Yet, I may say that the behaviour which the society and the culture consider as unethical may be accepted as ethically acceptable by the police sub-culture. Some human rights laws, in every sense, are intended to check the misbehaviour and unethical acts of police and human rights violations are now treated as crimes in India. Authority, power, muscles, ego-inflation, ego-swellings, human rights unfriendlly attitude, pseudo-authority etc., I believe, have been very potent factors in the genesis of police acts of immorality during justice administration. Such factors instinctively arouse anger and anger may cause acts which are unethical.

A police Code of Ethics has come into existence and in seeking a new ethics of police behaviour, therefore, we must not ourselves be dominated by the hitherto existed police sub-culture. The police must ask to themselves a question: "What moral rules are most likely to promote law enforcement and justice administration in a human rights friendly manner"? The answer to the question will make a new police sub-culture for the third millennium - and such a service will have a moral conscience different from what it is today and now. Police officers have the freedom to do many things in connection with their functions but they are not free to violate their moral code. Something done unethically may have short run success, but will not last for a long time. For example, police used to take people into custody and retain them incommunicado for some days. The procedure adopted by police has been resented against by the people and the Supreme Court of India in D.K. Basu V.State of West Bengal has given directives to police regarding the formalities to be observed when arrest is made. The directives contain more of morality and social sense of the police to be exhibited during their functionings.

Police Ethics and Human Relations

"Police do not need a priestly ethics" - said a police officer and I do not know what he really meant by priestly ethics. The advocates of this school of thought may say that there is something called "*Lawyers' ethics*". If so there must be *'business mens'* ethics, teachers' ethics, burglars' ethics, rapists'ethics etc. When he said that the police did not need a priestly ethics, he, probably meant that the priests required to be very honest, sincere, holy, committed etc. whereas the police did not want to be so. I can not agree with his views as I can not find different types of honesty. Honesty means onething and it means the samething for the priest, police and thief. To split honesty into many like thief's honesty, priest's honesty etc. is not understandable. Likewise ethics can not be and should not be split into many.

Suppose a pickpocket picks the pocket of another, people say that he commits pickpockting – an immoral and criminal act. Suppose again that a policeman does the samething. The people say the samething about the police. Perhaps, they become uncharitable when they comment on the policeman here, for people expect the policeman to prevent pocket picking and not to commit it.

Human relations with the police may not develop well if the people find the police behaving without ethical norms being respected. People keep away from corrupt policemen, avoid policemen who speak indecently, shun away from policemen who have immorality just like they do so with people in other walks of life. If at all the police enforce laws, investigate crimes and do many other things for people, and if they do not do them strictly following the moral principles. then they will not get due approval for what they do. Once a few policemen organized raids in a night, but allegations were there that they insulted/abused women. The press, people and media raised their protest against the police actions. People may, as indicated earlier, tolerate crimes but will not tolerate police immorality. Once a police officer, when he wrote the mahazar, stole some valuables and misappropriated them. No doubt, it was a crime to do so, but more than that, it was an immoral act. People do not want to associate with immoral acts. People do not want to associate with immoral people whatever may be their position in life and the same approach is taken by the people in the case of policemen too. Police - people relations suffer a lot.

Ethics and ethical principles of the higher ups become a topic of discussion among the subordinates and in the public. If the top level administration is not ethics - conscious, then, it is likely that it affects the lower levels and the lowest levels. An ethics - conscious administration will certainly make an ethics – conscious service. Some top level officers do anything/many things to get an extention in service - may be for one month, or, for one year. People under them watch everything when these extention - mongering officers do and speak 'this and that'. A director general of police initiated disciplinary actions against many whom he did not like and he did it just before he retired on superannuation. His unethical action was severely criticized by many in the department and the people felt relief when they saw him retired from service. Another director general of police gave "mass pardon" in disciplinary proceedings and irrespective of the morality or immorality of his decision, he has been remembered with gratitude. Many officers/men offered thanks giving prayers to the Almighty for the decision the director general took for those who worked under him. By such a decision, he made it clear to all that the department was not against anyone. He also reminded everyone to be more concerned about duties and more committed in the work. The good work done by a person is always remembered and the bad work is always condemned. Likewise, law enforcement with ethics is appreciated and the same without ethics is looked down upon.

Police Ethics and Political Praxis

In a democracy, the police can not function without political interference. Political interference comes to police to see that the police do things in a just way or to do things in an unjust way.The police do not give an asssurance to people that they will do everything justly amidst and in spite of political interference. Why? Police officers can not do so, because they are very much dependent on politicians for their position and functionings. Politicians do many things for their existence and survival in a political party. Some people say that they may do anything if it is advantageous to them. If that is true, then ethics may not have any existence or survival value among may politicians. If politicians having no ethics come to police stations, then they may insist the police to do many things in an unethical manner. Police functionaries vulnerable to political interference yield to political wishes and whims.

Police ethics and political ethics – can they go together? Some say that political ethics is and should be different from police ethics. I do not know what do they mean by police ethics and political ethics. Ethics is one and there is no question of a double morality in justice administration. With political interference, the police must do justice and without political interference too, the police must do the same thing. For, justice is one and in the ultimate analysis is the same in politics and in police. No police officer should behave to people in a human rights unfriendly manner even if the political interference is very severe.

How can we divide ethics into many divisions like political, police, public, private, legal etc. If we divide ethics into many divisions, then we may have to apply different scales to each one of them and I do not know how is it possible to do so?

Every politician is a policeman and every policeman is a politician and they become one and the same if they have the same ethical conscience. Some police officers do not welcome political interference in their work. Why? For, they can not do things as the politicians want. Why? Their ethical conscience may be against the political (Whim). The ethical police conscience, I feel, will be perfect if it comes from an upright conscience.

Sometimes, it may not be so. Politician's conscience may be perfect if it comes from an upright conscience. An upright conscience, whether it be of a politician or of a police officer, is upright and therefore there can not be any difference or distinction between the two. The political option, the police option, the justice option, the morality option , the social option – all of them will be one and the same or must be so in the ultimate analysis – at the highest level where justice is to be administered. Police option, politician's option and justice option – all will have the denominator "Ethics Option". This common denominator decides everything - the righteousness, the legality, the lawfulness, the justice etc. Both politics and police are public responsibilities which can not, in a democracy, afford to operate in a manner each one (police or politician) desires - i.e. basing on police ethics or politicians' ethics. Police should not look at the politician as one who has no morality or moral conscience. Likewise, the politician must not view the police officer as one having no morality or moral consciousness. Both have ethical conscience and precisely, therefore, they must try to see that they work together with an upright conscience which is the right conscience.

An Ideal World of Ethics and a Practical World of Ethics

Police officers, sometimes, make attempts to have a distinction between an ideal world of ethics and a practical world of ethics. According to them, there is a lot of gap between "ought to" and "is" in police work. An ethically correct strategy may not be practically possible in police. "Ideality Versus Reality - how can they be reconciled in police work? I think that every law is something in "ideality" and the policeman tries to enforce the 'ideal law' into practical reality. If this is true in the case of State's laws, the same is true in the case of ethical laws. One may enforce ethical law in accordance to the dictates of his upright conscience. And that will be the perfect enforcement of ethical laws - ideally and practically. Necessity may lead the police to do many things which reason does not allow. Some of the actions thus taken or executed by police may become necessary crimes. What can be done then? A moralist, I am afraid, may argue that the necessities and circumstances alone should not determine police actions. When a police officer acts, he acts, and he acts responsibly and ethically. We can not blame the circumstances, necessities, helplessness etc. to be responsible for the actions we do. No doubt, necessity has no law. But, one can not make everything as "necessary" for obtaining ethical immunity in unethical acts.

Some people, I feel, still think that a policeman's job is not for those who do not want to get it dirtied. In other words, good people do not opt for police jobs. I do not know the logic and rationale behind such arguments. For, I, for one, think that police job is one in which a man having an upright conscience can do a great deal of wonderful human services. But, doubtlessly, the acts of many policemen so far created an impression among the people that they could be a group of people who could commit a variety of wicked acts without any ethics and moral considerations. I do not argue that the people are wrong in entirety in their impressions, yet behind their impressions, there are many police officers/men who are morally gem-like.

Every police officer/man must be moral and there arises no question of having a double morality or special morality for police officers. This argument for "double morality" is rejected long ago. Again, "the police is a special job and therefore the policemen have a special morality". This too is a discarded concept for reasons discussed above. Police behaviour must be determined not on the basis of a double morality or of a special morality but on the basis of an upright conscience which police officers have or should have. Police training should aim at developing an upright conscience in police officers/men. Common people judge the police by their appearance than by reality. Yes, it was so in the past. Today, people evaluate the police by reality than appearance. In olden dags, people were not very much concerned about the means the police took provided the end (result) was good. But, today, the people say that the end must be good and the means too must be human rights friendly. The concepts of just justice, equal justice, total justice etc. are in vogue now. A police officer who commits immoral acts in justice administration may say like Macbeth "a little water will cleanse us of this deed." But later, the same officer may lament: "Will these hands never be clean". Why? This is called the prick of conscience. The morality of police actions must not be judged only from an external point of view of success. The success in police work has many dimensions and the social consequences, human happiness, just justice administration, human rights projection, morality of the acts etc. are just a few among the various dimensions. Immediate success of a police action must also be weighed against its ultimate consequences in justice administration and police-people interactions. Police work for the people and the realm of police may be a twilight zone where ethical, social, legal, constitutional issues meet and a police officer who is able to see the ethical dimensions of what he does, will certainly, be rewarded. It is not always possible to decide the ethics of police actions from an external point of view. Hence, the social, legal and police consequences of an act must be taken as a scale of its morality than the hidden motive. Suppose, for instance, a suspect taken into custody by the police subsequently is found dead in a police station. From the external point of view, it may be a natural death, a suicide, a death by an accident or a homicide in police custody. What is the social, legal, and police consequences of a death in police custody. It becomes necessary for the police to convince the people that it is a natural death. The morality of custodial death affects police-people interactions. Belief and behaviour, I see in police go together. If a police officer who believes in morality behaves morally, if he does not, it means that he does not. If a police officer believes in double morality or special morality he behaves accordingly.

Police ethics has not, so far, been a topic of police interest. But today, it assumes a greater interest than many other issues in police work. We had the British police, democracy's police, ruling government's police, law enforcing police, law abiding police etc. but one wonders whether or not we have had a "moral police" or a police respecting ethical values! The police has to be moral and that is necessary for the police to become human. The police of the third millennium must be armed with the wisdom of the police of today but remain free from their wickedness, malice and immorality.

Police Ethics and Police Discipline

An ethical definition of discipline is not seen in police literature. The reason probably is that discipline, as understood today in police, is not intended to make the police ethical in life. A *sena model hierarchy,* as we have today, needs to learn the words of command to administer more easily the police personnel than extending police service to people. Attention position, saluting, complimenting etc. are seen more in interpersonnel relations than in police people interactions. How is the impact of police discipline upon police morality? I think that the discipline taught at present has nothing much to do with police ethics. It is the "*disciplined policeman*"(?) who is caught for corruption, custodial rape and concoction of evidence before the courts of law. It is the so name "disciplined policeman" who is convicted by courts of law for offences committed by him. It is the so called "disciplined policeman" who is exposed in the media as ethics unfriendly. Police discipline and police morality are one and the same. If you are indisciplined, it means you don't respect moral laws. A person who honours moral law can not become discipline unfriendly.

When I speak of discipline as an ingredient of police ethics, I am not thinking of "yes sir, no sir" sub-culture in police. "A parade ground discipline" may inculcate such behavioural patterns among the police personnel. But, police ethics is evaluated from what they show to people. While policemen condemn the acts which are criminal and committed by people, it is seen that the same policemen condone the same type of acts committed by their colleagues, subordinates and associates. Policemen condemn causing of simple hurt by people – they also condemn theft by people. But how many of them condemn torture in police stations? How many of them condone such tortures? I know a retired police officer who claimed to be highly ethical taking a tolerating attitude to police torture when suspects were questioned. So long as that officer continued to tolerate police torture, he could only do harm to police ethics. By seniority and position, he occupied senior posts in the hierarchy. He was to teach ethics and ethical principles to police personnel working under him. The impact has been that one of the junior officers who found such tolerating attitude from the higher ups recently told in a private conversation that "*even* 'so and so' *allowed torture in police custody*". I think that he got wrong signals from the officer who tolerated torture in police stations.

Policemen of all ranks must be taught to respect human rights and dignity. They must be taught that no law allows policemen to employ torture on a suspect. They must be taught that every law they enforce has an ethic behind it. And they must be taught that any human rights violation is a crime under law and an evil under ethics. It is obvious that all unethical acts are acts against police discipline and are more destructive to the police than to the victims of unethical acts of police. How can an unethical policeman be disciplined in life? – show discipline in his work? If he appears to be disciplined, surely, he is a hypocrite.

One reason, I can boldly say, for the growth of unethical behaviour in police is the influences the trainers and superior ranks in police exert on the new entrants to service. Of course, by association, learning, imitation, suggestion, identification etc. each one may master unethical behavioural patterns. Nevertheless, lack of good models and supervision by morally upright personnel have a greater influence on the new entrants. Moulding period is very important and the mould decides the type of person in police service. If the mould and the moulding agencies are moral, then the finished product too will be moral, otherwise not. Every trainee must be taught that nothing can justify an act unless one keeps an ethics to do it justly. No police officer has a moral right over the moral right of a citizen. Moral instructions are given to children in schools and likewise, moral instructions must be imparted to every trainee to police service.

One of the defects of traditional policing is its individualism- i.e. the police officer seeks for individual success in what he does. The individualism of police functionaries had its value when administration of criminal justice was the only objective. Today, administration of criminal justice alone is not the objective of police performance of duties. Police are to perform their duties under an equal justice system wherein victim justice including justice to the victims of abuse of power and misuse of authority is taken into account under a just justice system. Today, we need more a total justice than an individual conception of success in police work. During the British rule, the police could not alter the methods of justice administration. For, they were doing everything for satisfying a foreign power in India. But after independence, the police do things to satisfy the people for whose welfare the service is maintained. In the new democratic set up, the police should adopt new strategies and methods for the greater welfare of the people. The good things the police do must be appreciated by the people. Justice today has many dimensions and ultimately and essentially, it is for the people and for nobody else.

Police in India belong to the largest democracy in the world and precisely must be a model to all police services in other democracies. The hitherto maintained feeling that police need not very much take into account the ethics of their action has no existence now and therefore a generation is coming up and it holds the view that police ethics is as important as police laws in a democracy. I want to suggest that a police service with an ethical outlook-sufficiently bold and conscious of its ethical responsi-bilities-will have a stronger existence in the next millennium. A good police service, as the people today conceive it, demands a multitude of social and ethical values. No police service can be extended or ensured to people without honouring the social and ethical values. The good police service is and should be inspired by principles guided by morality. For example, policemen doing services at a site of natural clamity must do them with human dignity and with respect for human dignity. The same principle is applicable in crime investigation, law and order management or similar jobs taken up by the police. Behind every police action, there must be a human conscience guided by upright moral values. If that is not there, then there will be custodial violence, custodial death and miscarriage of justice in police work. We had enough of them in the past and that might be the unique reason why policemen did not get due appreciation for the hazarduous work they do. The policemen should not think that the suspects, the accused, the detinues and so on are of inferior clay and their sufferings do not matter much during the administration of just justice. Even if they are criminals or detected to have committed crimes, they do not surrender their human rights to the mercy of the policemen. Violating human rights to establish human rights is not the method to establish human happiness and social welfare. To build up good police service, the police must - and no one else - build up self - control and sympathy for others. There is no short cuts to become human in police service.

Why I am not a Policeman?

I am repeating the title *again and again* and I do so because I do not want a man to take up the job without understanding the role and purpose of being a policeman in a democracy. The basic principle in policing is that the police want to create an order in society – a society consisting of nice people - people who do not want to violate laws - laws which are enacted for harmonious living. It goes without saying that the creators of nice people must be nice in their interactions. Who must be nicer – the people or the police? Necessarily the police must be nicer and they are trained to be nice to others. To be nice to others is a strength - a force with rifles and lathies can not guaranteenicity to people who commit crimes. If people do not commit crimes, then the police may not be required. If police commit crimes, then who will be able to check them? People think that enforcement crimes are found rampant in police sub-culture and they can be checked if the police perform their duties with an ethical conscience.

I do not know what is meant by 'police justice' and I do not know who invented that phrase. When I enter into a police station, then I see people in half-nakedness, then I do not think that it is *police justice* to keep people in that way. I can see it only as a human right violation and nothing more. Before any amount of justification brought to convince me about the 'justness' in so doing, I may still think that the procedure is nothing but miscarriage of justice. Police station is a public facility and it must be decent enough for the public to come whenever they want. Handcuffs, lock-ups, lathies and rifles do not make a police station. It is the people who work therein and if they are morally upright, then it will be the *holy of holies* for administering justice–not police justice–but equal justice under law.

Every society gets a police service which it deserves. This is a forelone concept. Today, people say that every policeman makes a society he wants. His capacity to make people law abiding is enviable. The beat constable knows everyone living there and he speaks to each one of them. People talk to him as a friend, guide and philosopher provided he is a person possessing human qualities – an upright conscience and a human face. It follows without saying that only those people possessing human qualities, upright conscience and human face can serve and survive as policemen in the third millennium.

7

Life in Police Service: What I Hear and See?

What about the family life of the police personnel? Do they marry at the appropriate age? Do they enjoy a family life? Do their children come up in life? Are they able to fulfil their role and responsibilities as the heads of the family? I do not know whether or not any studies have been conducted on this, yet many policemen - constables in particular - make complaints that they have many difficulties to have a pleasant life. Why? I asked some and they say that the 24 hour job creates a lot of problems. They are, in law, on duty for twenty four hours and it is a Damocles' Sword for many. If not found when called for duty, they may have to face disciplinary actions.

Once a policeman, always a policeman and everywhere a policeman — is it true? I asked the questions to the wives of certain policemen and I got the response "yes" — meaning that they are policemen even at home. The position gets changed when one goes higher and higher in ranks. Officers of the higher strata get married to women who are economically well to do. Owing to the dowry system, it so happens that some rich and affluent people purchase young police officers from the marriage market. Police officers who enjoy social status and authority by job (not economically) thus become all on a sudden - over night - very affluent by marriage. With their salary or legitimate income, a good number of them may not be able to live a luxurious life. They may not be able to maintain an expensive wife-a luxury in every sense. In order to do so, they either become corrupt or heavily depend upon their fathers-in-law who may look after them well if they abide by the orders they issue. If they reject their orders and guidance, they become hostile to their fathers-in-law. On the contrary, if they listen, they may have to work like a slave to the wishes and whims of their fathers-in-law. In both cases, they become unhappy. Any hundreds of such cases can be taken from police departments. Official authority, position, status of the police officers and the conscious or unconscious effects of them in their talk and behaviour irritate the rich and affluent wives who think that their husbands are commodities purchased by their parents for their happy living. There is lack of understanding and mutual respect. They fail to the appreciate the fact that the functions in the family must be exercised to promote mutality in love.

Police constables are educated now. Yet the fact remains that they do not have the social status which officers in police service get. Lack of social status affects their marriage alliance. Nevertheless, some of them marry educated women and quite a few of them are employed too. Educated constables, generally, are found to be disinclined to take up traditional police jobs like sentry duty, escort duty, process serving, beat and traffic controls etc. They prefer to do no-police job like office work or works of similar nature which do not have high public visibility. If the wives are better educated than the constables, I am told, the police constables feel less in front of them. Police women have extreme difficulties to find out a suitable marriage partner for them. I understand that the people who marry police women do not like them to go for night duties. The women constables who are asked to do night duties are disinclined to do the job. There may be little or no facilities to do the job by women. Some women constables complain that they have to sleep in the same room where women of ill repute or notorious sexual contacts are retained. At a time sex-workers make their special claims, the police women find it extremely difficult to touch them as they are afraid of contamination. All these and many mental blocks affect their family life.

Young and unmarried sub-inspectors get better marriage alliance and financial position after marriage. But today, owing to the recruitment of sub-inspectors at a higher age, many sub-inspectors are already married when they are enlisted to police service. Some of them feel that they would have got better marriage alliance if they would have married after their entry to service. These feelings do affect their marital life. Sub-inspectors are transferred often so much so that they are forced to lead "broken family" life and their children's education is thus adversely affected. The problems connected with family dislocation, difficulties with children's education, frequent transfers, settlement uncertainties, maintaining of double establishments, unnecessary expenditure come more in the case of middle level police functionaries in the general executive branch of the police than in the case of armed reserves/armed batallions. Inadequate number of family quarters adjacent to police establishments, unbearable rent to hire out family accommodation at the place of work, insufficient house rent allowances etc. multiply the problems and difficulties connected with family budgets and financial well-being. I have seen that many police officers constructed houses for their residence only at the fag end of their career whereas people employed in other services do the same when they are in the age group of 35-40 or when they complete 10-15 years of service. Quite often this is not possible for police personnel at the middle, lower or lowest strata in the police hierarchy. The life style of the policemen-particularly the constabulary-is far away from being satisfactory. How many children of the constables come up in life-educationally? economically? job-wise? A casual observation shows that many of them do not go up high in achievement scales? How many children of the middle level police functionaries come up in life?

Owing to the frequent absence of the father at home, inability of the father to provide care for their children, family management by a sort of police discipline at home, children's ego formation in a police style affect their personality development and settlement i n life. Higher and highest level officers settle their children better in life and this may be owing to their official position, financial stability etc. Nevertheless, it is observed recently that the children of high ranking police officers do experience adjustment problems with their husbands. Some of them reach to the extent of dissertion, separation or divorce. Whatever that be, family life, the pleasures and pains connected with the family life affect the nature of police functions.

Within the department, there may be harassment and victimization. Disciplinary inquiries are plenty and there may not be many in the middle level of police administration who are not subjected to disciplinary actions once, twice or many times in their career. Look at the face of the policeman, then one can see how happy he is in the department! Call him and ask him: "what makes you disturbed?". His answer will be: "I am facing a departmental inquiry". Ask him more about it then he may narrate the hardships connected with the conduct of disciplinary inquiries. Generally, the policemen complain that the inquiry officer does not know how to conduct the inquiry in a quasi-judicial way. There is undue-extremely undue delay in the conduct and finalization of the inquiry. What is more?

The life becomes miserable and some of the policemen commit suicide or take to drinks and drugs. "I was a police officer who was not ever corrupt in my life" — said a circle inspector once. He continued:"But, I was once placed under suspension. The suspension continued for 1 1/2 years. Nobody bothered about me. I had to look after my family and I did so by selling my valuables and borrowing money from available sources. I learnt a lesson then. '*Make money when you can*' and afterwards I started receiving corruption money. Now I have no difficulty to manage myself /my family if at all I am suspended for years together". I understand that it is not an isolated case. There are many who have become corrupt after a suspension or a departmental inquiry being initiated against them. One retired director general of police once made a casual remark: "so and so was an upright officer. But, once he was chargesheeted for causing custodial death and went to jail. Afterwards, when he joined back the department and occupied important positions in public undertakings he made a lot of money. Now, he has nothing to worry". He further said: "Make fortunes as much as you can when you are in service. If you are caught, spend half of the fortune and get a clean escape. This has become the style of functionings now". I am not interested to discuss the ethical issues connected with his observation, nevetheless I feel that some police functionaries move things as per the above directives as they think that there is a lot of truth in what he says. There are police officers who have made real fortunes by being in police department. They might have come to join the department with a brief-case and a pair of dress. They might retire from service as wealthy king and of course, they might have faced a few departmental inquiries from which they managed to get out uninjured owing to their financial stability or political patronage. Some police officers feel that political patronage can be purchased whereas poverty, prayers and good will can not purchase it. Police officers who are caught for corruption and for causing miscarriage of justice occupy important positions on their reinstatement back and this happens because of their political patronage. How do they manage it?

What about the interpersonnel relationship? A sort of rank based or unit based relationship can not offer harmony. If paper reports are true, one may notice that officers/men in the general executive fight against the officers/men in armed batallions/reserves and vice versa. Litigations and litigations on service matters are filed before the administrative tribunals and high courts. Why? Promotion prospects are lacking at the lower and lowest levels and they are brightest at the higher and highest levels.

Disparity in salary, perks, privileges, comforts may be a lot and the people at the lower levels see it. They can not tolerate it and they speak about it in silent language. They repress their feelings and express them in many ways. Depression, rejection, aggression, withdrawal, tolerance etc.. may be the outcome in such situations. Many educated constables are there in police department and they express their reactions in an telligent manner.

What about the police welfare measures? National Police Commission has spoken about it. Police associations speak about it. Police men speak about it. But, what is coming out? Police welfare is linked with service conditions, career prospects, human comforts, promotional avenues, interpersonnel relationship, accommodation, housing, transfers, family benefit schemes, children's education, life style and social status of women and what not?A comprehensive programme for the police welfare must be chalked out without delay. Any welfare measures may not be effective if there is no free communication within the department.

I see many officers express "Muscle Ego" when they talk to associates and subordinates. They do not relax—relax to the least. This causes mental blocks for free communication. Rank consciousness consumes many so much so that the authoritarian rank consciousness overpowers even when personal contacts are made. Rank in police is important, but it is not everything in police administration. Interpersonnel relationship with a human face is a pre-requisite for any police welfare. The lower and the lowest ranks are taught in the parade ground that the slighest displeasure of the next higher rank can be a cause of disciplinary proceedings against anybody in service and it is understood that it has been taking place many a time in police administration. Higher ranks think that they alone can offer a good administration. But, the constables think that they can ensure better administration if they are taken into confidence and are interacted in a human way. Some police constables say: "Whoever had invented rank in police service did not think much about its connection with other ranks". I think that there is a point in that. Rank generally means a relative position or standing, but in police, it has a lot of meanings, inner meanings, egos, ego - projections, authority, authoritarian attitudes, privileges, perks and what not? The entire human relations are based on what ranks two people occupy in the hierarchy. The lower rank salutes the higher rank and the higher ranks must command salutes - but it seems that they demand salutes and that shows the nature of human relations. "On personal level, I do not have a rank as I am a civilian. People look at me on the basis of my basic pay and often equate me with a rank. Police officers who draw higher basic pay than what I have, used to look at me as their subordinates and I do not know how. In spite of my qualifications, achievements, academic merits, I see that certain officers "*looking down upon me*" and I used to feel pity at their ego - swellings and pasted vanities. A vehicle at one's disposal and the rank he holds makes him feel bigger than what he is and certainly, I do not have a police vehicle at my disposal. The reason is that a certain police officer under whom I worked thought that I should be ignored by denying a vehicle to me. I know that he has a lot of inferiority feelings in front of me and therefore I do not take serious note of it". The above feelings were expressed by a civilian member on the teaching faculty of a police training college in India and I could learn that there was frustration on his face. If this was so in the case of a civilian member of the faculty in a police college, things were worse in the case of police functionaries who did possess ranks in the hierarchy.

"Why I am not a Policeman?" — yes, I am not because I can not accommodate myself with the rank consciousness in police. Certain police officers say thus because they feel that they are chained by their ranks and are fixed in a rank. They are treated as '*someone or no one*' basing on their ranks and they say that a share of what they do are robbed by the higher ranks in service. A detection in a criminal case by a constable/sub-inspector may be reported in the press as if the entire work is done by all officers in the hierarchy—most unkindest cut of all. Policemen who have some conscience may say that there are many aching issues in police and such issues repel police officers not to be "*police officers*' although all of them are *policemen* in the hierarchy.

8

Why I am a Policeman ?

I have no first hand information when or whether the director general of police asks this question to himself. At the same time, many policemen honestly tell me that they never ask this question to them. For, they take it for granted that they are policemen. I thought of, once, asking this question to the director general of police directly, but did not. For, I did not know how he would react to my question. Sometimes, he might ignore my question or the question might irritate him. There was another possibility too. The question would make him to think and find an answer to my question: "Why I am a Policeman?"

There might be one thousand and one reasons for a person to opt for a police job. I am not interested to know about any of them. My question is : 'Why I am a Policeman?'. In other words, why do I continue as a policeman?'. Certainly, the call was conditional—i.e. if you wanted to be a policeman, then be a policeman. Once the condition was accepted, then telling "this or that" and not doing the police job as the policeman is expected to do is a deceit—a deceit to self and to others in society. Such a person is not a policeman, but a hypocrite in police uniform and he does maximum harm to the organization he represents and to the people.

"Why I am a Policeman?". The answer to the question may be seen in the chapter on police duties and responsibilities as given in Police Acts, laws, rules and standing orders. Those things can be studied by anybody and repeat them. My question is "what is written in your heart as the duties and responsibilities of a policeman?". I am more interested to hear that—than what is written on the pages of the printed books or statutes. You may be able to convince anybody that you are doing things in the right way. But, my question is : "can you convince yourself that you are doing everything in the right way?". If you can do so, you are very great. But, it is not that easy to do so. Self-convincing is the best convincing and how many policemen can do so? There is a greater policeman inside the police uniform and one should make attempts to convince the inner policeman—the human conscience—which is otherwise called an upright human conscience. Only a person who has received the right human formation can possess an upright human conscience. Does the director general have it? - does the constable have it? Suppose, if the constable has it and the director general does not have it, then, certainly the constable is superior to the director general of police.

Who is a policeman? I do not think that there is a proper definition or description for it. Some people say that a policeman is not a word; it is a paragraph and there is a lot of truth in that. Many policemen do not know it. They enter the service with some ulterior motives and they become poor policemen. A policeman is one who respects his dignity and the dignity of others. For, every man is equal in dignity to others—and the human person, unlike animals and things, can not be subjected to domination by others.

What is the policeman doing in society? He may be doing a lot of things—nothing if he does not have human qualities and desirable personality traits. How a thing is done assumes more importance than what is done by the policeman. Render police service with a "human face" and that must be the approach. Be human rights friendly to people. 'Policeman' contains '*man*' and the prefix has meaning only when 'man' means what it really means.

Man is the centre of the universe—*homocentric* — and everything moves around him. Policeman recognises this fact when he executes law or administers justice - justice of every description which I may enumerate again and again as criminal justice, victim justice, gender justice, social justice, human rights justice, just justice etc. under an equal justice system which offers total justice to the criminals, to the victims including victims of abuse of power/misuse of authority, to the society and to the justice system itself.

A policeman is not to administer or to aid the administration of "*wounded justice*" to people. People become helpless before the mammoth police system and suffer it. Things do not end there. People lose their trust on police and the distrusted policeman becomes a curse for the society—a liability for the people who retain him in service.

What is the purpose of being a policeman in society? The purpose is just one and that is police service—police service and police service alone. Service has only one meaning and police service has the same meaning which the service has—nothing more and nothing less. Police is not at all a Force in a democratic setup. If anybody thinks in that way—and I know that some directors general of police think so—it is a perverted thought and must be corrected. Like any other service, police too have limitations. Accept the limitations as they are and act accordingly. Man is limited in space and time and the policeman is in his uniform as well.

Police in uniform is highly visible and precisely therefore they must allow maximum transparency in police work. Be accountable to what is done under the uniform. Policeman, to repeat is a public servant and not a government servant. Susceptibility and vulnerability to pressures, introductions, temptations and recommendations is a sin against man and God - against humanity and heaven.

Police job with public participation is a novel idea that must yield good results. Police and people—both exist in a society. To exist means to co-exist. Police have no survival value without people. People may live with an organized police system as seen today, but the police can not live without the people. Ensure maximum good will, co-operation and participation from the people for the success of police work.

Police are moral and they ought to be so. Morality is not the monopoly of the moralists or if at all it is so, then each policeman is a moralist. Every law which the police enforce has a moral conscience behind it. This is applicable in all police activities from harassment to custodial deaths. Police must be open in their approach and openness makes police activities visible to all. The traditional police works get changed and the modalities are questioned and sometimes reacted against. Enforcement of law in a lawless manner, no doubt, might have been tolerated in the past, but such law enforcements marked by a mistaken sense of police responsibilities can not get public appreciation now and during the years to come. Police concept of law enforcement which has hitherto followed by certain police officers, sometimes, becomes a target of public attack blaming it to be the enforcement of the "strong" against the weak who have no choice but to submit.

Why I am a Policeman? This question can be answered only in the light of principles followed by the international community for whom there is no Indian police. Indian police is a part of the internatonal police and owing to the phenomenal development of the information technology, anything done by Indian police may assume international significance. The responsibilities entrusted to police must be done in a responsible way and not in an individualistic manner. Police authority can not become an authority leading to human rights violations. In such a situation, the police will be considered an enemy from whom the people will find out ways and means to defend themselves. Then, the police become a mass of individuals placed side by side to the individuals in society, but without any mutual bonds. As a control mechanism, police is an institution which must work in close association with the people. Police-people relations get significant importance in these days. Some kind of compromise between the police and the people become essential then. People and the police have common values and the effort must be to attain them for the larger interest of the society.

People can prevent the commission of crimes. They can maintain law and order. They can extend their full co-operation to police during the investigation of crimes. In all such situations, every man on the street is a policeman and he asks to himself: "Why I am a Policeman". He can, like a uniformed policeman in service, administer justice and also abort justice. The power and capacity of the people in policing the society, therefore, must be respected and recognized in all fairness by the police authorities. Policing the society is the people's job now and during the millennium.

Many policemen tell me that without them, people can be neither safe nor happy. I do not know what they mean by such a statement. As to the safety of man, I can speak from my personal experience. I am safe because I take safety measures by myself. I do not think that I am safe because the policemen work else - where in the city. Every society takes its own safety measures and the police is just one such safety measures which the society maintains at stupendous cost. As to happiness, I can not subscribe to the view that people are happy because the police are vigilant in their work. Amidst the policemen and in spite of them, there are many unhappy men in society. Even, some of the policemen are unhappy and dissatisfied and they commit suicide. The number of policemen committing suicide is on the increase. It goes, therefore, without saying that safety and happiness of people exist with or without the policemen and there is no meaning in claiming things which one does not deserve. Consequently, it follows: 'Without people, the police can not exist and with people, they can exist offering happiness and safety to their own lives and to the lives of others in society. Hence an attitude of 'let us work together for human safety and happiness' must be developed in every policeman!' "What have you done to the safety and happiness of the people?"— this question must be addressed to all people in society if the police want to police the society with public participation. I do not think that such an approach has assumed importance in police work today.

From my experience of two and half decades of service in police, I firmly believe that there must be a general mobilization of the new trends and a united effort to activate an orientation of police attitudes in the right direction. There is the immediate need to build a new culture of police service–new because it will be able to bring more people closer to police - new because it will enable the police to have a dialogue with people. Police must not separate their legal obligations and responsibilities from their social commitments and healthy human interactions with the public. Police subjectivism and their objectionable ways of behaviour must find natural death and decay. With clarity and determination, police must identify their sublime roles in a democratic society. The most fundamental step towards this cultural transformation lies in shaping of police personality which recognizes and respects human dignity and the inviolable worth of every human person. The essential connection between police and citizens must be cemented. The police and the people are inseparable-when one does not co-operate with the other, then there ceases to have any praiseworthy policing. There is the need for education about the value of police-people relations. It is an illusion to think that police can perform their duties without public participation. The work of educating on *policing with public participation* involves the training of police officers/men in responsible policing.

Why I am a Policeman? I am a policeman, because I can not be anybody else. I am a policeman, because I want to be a policeman. Iam a policeman because no one else can do the work which I do as a policeman. I am a policeman, because the people around me insist that I should continue as a policeman. There is a greater greatness in the greatness of being and becoming a great policeman.

Appendix

An Unknown Policeman's Diary*

This is the ***Diary*** of an unnamed policeman-certainly, he is not unfamiliar. He has thoughts and he expresses them, one after the other. He is amidst us. His ***Diary*** traces the thoughts, actions, reactions and interactions of an unknown policeman in Indian society. A lively exposition of a human mind in khaki uniform that will educate as well challenge.

Who is this unknown policeman? Is he the constable, the sub-inspector, the superintendent of police, the inspector general of police, the director general or all of them? Of course, the unknown policeman is a legion and he writes his diary. He writes what he sees around him.

He thinks "Why I am a Policeman?" — "Why I am not a Policeman?". He also thinks: "How should I be a Policeman?". He finds a lot of passages in Indian Scriptures and he thinks that these noble thoughts can effect correction in all people—including the police. He thinks that the essence of police service must be appreciated by policemen. Existence of police has no meaning if the essence is not well accepted.

This ***Diary*** of an unknown policeman will serve as an enlightenment and an aid to all who want to render police service to people in a democracy. Police moves to the twenty first century to the third millennium. They need wisdom which works for the

(*Not chronologically arranged)

good of people. However much the police may claim that they are doing marvellous services, they may have to endorse the view that they can achieve nothing if they do not possess a human conscience. "Human formation" is more important than police training, education and authority. The unknown policeman thinks for many from all angles and precisely therefore he must be listened to: "Why I am not a Policeman?" — "Why I am a Policeman?" — Both are important and both need answers.

This diary contains the wisdom of a policeman which, "I hope, will direct many generations through the right path to the right direction." That was a Sunday. I found him alone in the lockup. He was very sad. Yes, nothing is dearer to a person than his freedom in this world. I thought". He wrote on October 23, 1976.

❑ ❑ ❑ ❑ ❑

I am a policeman and certainly I can be kind to a suspect in a custodial facility. "May my life, each breath of life, the eyes, the ears, the speech, the mind, the soul and all other acts and deeds be put to the service of mankind" (Yajur Veda, 18,29). People have given me the police uniform to protect human dignity and precisely therefore everyone in police lockup must wear decent dress. Giving short loin clothes of news papers to cover the private parts of a man in police lockup is a human right violation. Yet, some do so. Why?
16-11-1976.

❑ ❑ ❑ ❑ ❑

Today, I am promoted as a deputy inspector general of police. I must be happy today. "Look at the staff-car with the flag and the star. Yes, a single star and thus I become a Flag Officer today. People look at my car, then my driver and then 'me' when I move around in my car".

"After wearing the new uniform-the uniform of a deputy inspector general of police-I must do my duties". In the Isha

Upanishad, it is written — "They who neglect their social duties for their individual life fall in darkness, and those who sacrifice their individuality for social popularity fall into greater darkness". 24-12-1976.

❑ ❑ ❑ ❑ ❑

The director general of police today conducted a conference and he spoke about detachment from politics and politicians' favours. I do not know whether or not the director general himself could claim that he could detach himself from politics and politicians' favours! In Gita III, 19, it is clearly written: "Therefore, without attachment, constantly perform action which is duty, for, by performing action without attachment man verily reaches the Supreme".
7-3-1977.

❑ ❑ ❑ ❑ ❑

Swamy Vivekanada said: "Let everyone do the best he can for realizing his own ideal. The apple tree should not be judged by the standard of the oak nor the oak by that of the apple tree". Witnesses, complainants, suspects, informers, women, children, politicians, journalists and many more people come to police stations. Are they treated alike or differently? How should each one of them be treated in a human rights friendly way? This must be taught to the constables and to officers. For, Swamiji Vivekanada again said: "A man must not be judged by the nature of his duties, but by the manner in which he does them". 13-10-1977.

❑ ❑ ❑ ❑ ❑

I see many police officers-including constables — are highly educated. But, they do not behave, sometimes, as educated people. They use filthy language and epithets to people. Why? They need further education and let them understand: "The object of education is the freedom of the mind, which can only be achieved through the path of freedom-though freedom has its risks

and responsibility as life itself has" (Tagore). A university degree or a diploma or an enlistment of a person to a particular cadre or service does not and can not make him educated.
20-11-1977.

Today, a M.L.A. said in the State Legislature: "A person goes as a man to a police training college and he returns as a policeman". What does he mean by that statement? He means that the man returns as a policeman who, according to him, is a tormentor of people. He returns as a muscle-man and he tortures people. Is the M.L.A. fully correct? Gandhiji once said : "A school or a college is a sanctuary where there should be nothing that is base or unholy. Schools and colleges are factories for the making of character". Is his observation true as far as police training schools/colleges/academies are concerned? I reserve my comments.
24-11-1977.

❑ ❑ ❑ ❑ ❑

Jawaharlal Nehru thought: "Education has mainly two aspects, the cultural aspect which makes a person grow and the productive aspect which makes a person do things. Both are essential. I want to ask: "does the police training has the above mentioned two aspects"?
29-11-1977.

❑ ❑ ❑ ❑ ❑

The police are always critical against their culture and behaviour-even when their productive aspect is enviable. Perhaps, there exists no proper atmosphere in police sub-culture for the development of a desirable culture of behaviour. "If you just help in creating an atmosphere, the rest will be done by the atmosphere itself. Even the wingless leaves rise high like birds when a powerful storm comes" (Vinoba Bhave).
14-3-1978.

❑ ❑ ❑ ❑ ❑

Human Right. The concept is of recent origin. That is what the Director General of Police tells now. I think that he needs more information about it. In Rig Veda 5,60,5, it is written: "There is none high or low among you. You are all brethren and therefore strive all together to attain prosperity".
11-6-1994.

❑ ❑ ❑ ❑ ❑

"If we look through all the earth

Men we see have equal birth

Made in one great brotherhood,

Equal in the sight of God; the good

Food or caste or place of birth,

Can not alter human worth. (Swami Ram Tirath)

19-9-1995.

❑ ❑ ❑ ❑ ❑

Do the Police reflect over that sublime thought? If not, they must. For, again in Rig Veda 2,13, 2 it is written: "All who can walk are equally entitled to the use of paths and roads".
27-10-1996.

❑ ❑ ❑ ❑ ❑

"God watches the acts of all" (Rig Veda 1,11,4) and this consciousness must be there when anything is done. 'Law with a conscience' and law enforcement with a human conscience must be there when crimes are investigated. In such a system, there is no scope for any sort of concoction of evidence and production of false or tutored witnesses. Allegations are there that the police concoct evidence and today too, I read such an allegation in the press. "Repel evil-minded persons" (Yajur Veda, 19-38)
20-4-1982.

❑ ❑ ❑ ❑ ❑

Today, when I was patrolling the jurisdiction with a police team, I heard my colleagues using foul words and filthy expressions. They need refinement in behaviour and words and I remembered: "A person who does not speak a word and whose face is always furrowed with frowns, becomes an object of hatred with all creatures. Absention from agreeable speaches makes him so. That person who, upon beholding others, addresses them first and does so with smiles, succeeds in making everyone gratified with him.

Even gifts, if not made with agreeable speeches, do not delight the recipients, like rice without curry. If even the possessions of men be taken away with sweet speeches, such sweetness of behaviour succeeds in reconciling the robbed". This is what is seen in Shanti Parva, in Mahabharata (84, 5-8) and the police need to know and appreciate the Indian thoughts.
27-7-1989.

❑ ❑ ❑ ❑ ❑

I used to think: "Why does the police fail to have a good image among the public even after 50 years' of democracy's policing in the Country?" Policemen admit this fact and yet, they fail to understand that a man can become good only by his good deeds, and bad by his bad deeds. Custodial violence, human rights violations, registration of false cases, use of excessive force etc. make the service unenviable before the public.
19-11-1996.

❑ ❑ ❑ ❑ ❑

Wisdom comes from anyone and the rank does not have much to do with the wisdom and knowledge one has. But, in hierarchical pattern of administration, a constable's knowledge is not well recognized. In Manu Smriti (2,239), it is written : "If nectar is mixed with poison, poison should be removed and nectar obtained; a piece of sound advice should be taken even from small child; gold should be picked up even if it be in filth". The higher ups must come down and learn from the lower ranks, if

that is necessary. A head constable may teach a sub-inspector/ an assistant superintendent of police. "Learn wisdom whosoever teaches it. Consider over its merit and never mind the quality of the teacher" (Hazrat Ali). A director general of police who is ignorant may be respected? within his jurisdiction, but a constable who is a scholar will be respected everywhere-down the years.
20-10-1991.

❑ ❑ ❑ ❑ ❑

What do the policemen do? They do a lot of jobs. Their acts lead to their habit. Is there something called police habit? Yes, there is and their habits lead to police behaviour. Police behaviour-what is it? It forms character and police character makes police personality. What is police personality? Many do not know it although everybody speaks about it.

Police habit, their behaviour–their character and personality make the police cultured and the culture is what the police are in a society.
10-3-1981.

❑ ❑ ❑ ❑ ❑

"Physical well being is an essential part of human well being"-said Dr. Radhakrishanan. With physical well-being there must be the intellectual and moral well-being and that is what is lacking in police?. Where the police are justly just, they radiate peace and harmony in society. Every policeman works in a world which he has created for himself and for others. Be neat and honest.
7-7-1997.

❑ ❑ ❑ ❑ ❑

Police is not only a man-oriented service but also it is a civilization and a culture. I do not think that many in police service feel so. Why? The reason might be that the police have been the servants of the ruling party in power till yesterday. To some extent even today, some men/officers think so.
21-2-1980.

❑ ❑ ❑ ❑ ❑

Why I am a policeman? I used to ponder over it. I think that a policeman can do the right thing at the right time at any cost if he wants to do so. That is what makes me to wear police uniform amidst the people who criticize the police, often, destructively and in spite of many criticisms. Sri. Buddha said: "There is no one in the world who is not blamed" and the police is certainly a service which may become a victim of blame at any time. It does not disuade me from functioning as a policeman.
17-1-1980.

❑ ❑ ❑ ❑ ❑

Today, I saw my superior-a deputy superintendent of police rejoicing. He found that one of his accused was convicted for life imprisonment. No doubt, it is a moment of the greatest triump for him! But, Gandhiji says that "the hour of the greatest triumph is the hour of the greatest humility". Police job, I think, can be described in a simple way-i.e. do the right thing for the greater benefit of people.
19-3-1985.

❑ ❑ ❑ ❑ ❑

Disciplinary justice-and that is what disciplinary authorities say when they initiate departmental actions against subordinates. Sometimes, actions are initiated for nothing-or for something that is the result of hostility, vengeance, jealousy, vindictiveness etc. "I am a policeman-and-hence I suffer it" this is the attitude some of my colleagues take when they become victims of disciplinary injustice. Kautilya said: "Ignorance and absence of discipline are the cause of man's troubles".
29-9-1999.

❑ ❑ ❑ ❑ ❑

Today, one of my colleagues committed suicide and he was given a burial with police honour. A few days ago, a police officer had a natural death and he too was given a burial with police honour. Yes, "death is thus an inescapable law of existence,

ordained for the good of the world. It is not true wisdom to be impatient with death or to grieve immoderately for those who die" (Mahabharata). I wish every policeman to think-reflect over the death of people in police custody and of their own death.
18-8-1982.

❑ ❑ ❑ ❑ ❑

Who accompanies man in death? I ask this question always and I think that "Dharma" alone can and will accompany a man in death. "Death is certain for everybody that is born, this death for which there is no remedy" (Srimad Bhagavata)
19-8-1982.

❑ ❑ ❑ ❑ ❑

"I know that the day will come when my sight of this earth shall be lost, a life will take its leave in silence, drawing the last curtain over my eyes"-Tagore said so in Gitanjali and what noble thought indeed!
20-8-1982.

❑ ❑ ❑ ❑ ❑

I heard a very senior officer uttering filthy words to his subordinates. Wounds inflicted by words remain painful as long as one lives (Devayani in Mahabharata) and the rank which blinds his eyes does not tell him that truth—"Beware of the anger of the tongue and control they tongue" (Dhammapada, 17)
9-9-1987.

❑ ❑ ❑ ❑ ❑

"Reverence to the great ones, reverence to the lesser ones. Reverence to the young, reverence to the old" (Rig Veda, I, 27, 13) and I add —

Reverence to the informers, to the

Complainants to the witnesses,

Reverance to the suspects,

accused, recidivists,

Reverance to the juveniles,

girls and women, to the

old and infirm, Reverence to all with

whom the police have

interactions.

11-12-1995.

❑ ❑ ❑ ❑ ❑

"Violence is suicide"-Gandhiji said and violence in police stations? What is it?
27-1-1981

❑ ❑ ❑ ❑ ❑

Vivekananda Swamiji said:

"Arise, awake, stop not till the goal is reached".

"No great work can be done without sacrifice"

"Look not back,. but forward".

And the policeman may reflect over them.

6-7-1984.

❑ ❑ ❑ ❑ ❑

The press today accused the police of using excessive force on people. Why does the press accuse the police? I think that still the police do not accept: "Strength does not come from physical capacity. It comes from an indomitable will" (Gandhiji)
17-3-1979.

❑ ❑ ❑ ❑ ❑

"Civility is a beauty of behaviour"-Tagore said and I tell it to my friends, superiors, subordinates and equals in police. " A genuine courtesy is a creation, like pictures and music"-again Tagore said and I repeat it.
1-1-1999.

❑ ❑ ❑ ❑ ❑

About a greedy man, Uttradhain Sutra (9,48) reads: "If there are million moutains like Himalayas of gold, even then the greedy man can not feel satisfied, because desire is unending like the firmament". I think that it is applicable to all corrupt officers and unjust administrators of justice. "One should not secure wealth by falsehood and other sinful acts" (Manu Smriti, 4.11). 31-12-1998.

❑ ❑ ❑ ❑ ❑

"All the gains and wealth that are in the three worlds, all the women of beauty, all the clothes and jewels, all these do not satiate even one greedy person.... The one who controls one's senses and has no craving is the one who is really happy and contented with a little. The unsatisfied man has no end of worries; the riches of the three worlds can not make him happy" (Sankaradeva) and I had this thought when I saw a police officer who amassed a lot of wealth from his service when he was cremated today.
17-3-1986.

❑ ❑ ❑ ❑ ❑

Serenity of mind, kindness, sympathy, self-control, honesty, loyalty, devotion to work, sincerity of motive-they are called the qualities of police service today and for the years to come.
28-10-1989.

❑ ❑ ❑ ❑ ❑

Knowledge can not spring up by any other means than enquiry, just as the perception of things is impossible without light (Sankaracharya: A parokshnubhuti II). Investigation of crime is a probe into for finding out the truth, but how well crimes are investigated? In any case, many cases are acquitted by courts and if that is the fact, what is the meaning of being or becoming a police investigator?
11-4-1980.

❑ ❑ ❑ ❑ ❑

Sri. Buddha said: "The smell of flowers goes only with the wind, but the fame of good men goes even against the wind". Likewise good policemen live even after their death, and bad policemen die even when they live. A few directors general of police are not heard after their retirement whereas some policemen are honoured even after their death. In Panchatantra, one reads: "Do the right, the right, the right till the breath of death; shun the wrong although the right leads to death or breath".
10-10-1981.

❑ ❑ ❑ ❑ ❑

"From greed comes grief from grief comes fear"-says Dhammapada. Greedy policemen live a life of grief and fear.
7-1-1993.

❑ ❑ ❑ ❑ ❑

Dhammapada says: "A man is not a supporter of the law because he talks too much.... he is the supporter of the law who never neglects the law". How many police officers/men obey the laws? If they obey the laws, then there is no meaning in speaking about lawless law enforcement or enforcement crimes. Some top level functionaries fight among themselves for the chairs and positions. They wash the dirty linen in public and they claim to be leaders!
20-11-1979.

❑ ❑ ❑ ❑ ❑

Any authority is transitory and power is temporary. But the top levels--not even the middle levels-not at all the lower levels-understand it. They think that they enjoy their power and authoirty eternally and they do not have death. Misuse of authority or abuse of power must not become a habit. For, Sri. Ramakrishna says: "The heart of a wicked man is like curled hair. It remains stright when pulled end to end but again assumes its former shape". 30-12-1987.

❑ ❑ ❑ ❑ ❑

Muscles, lathies, rifles, handcuffs, power and authority — All of them are meaningful for those who respect laws and have self-esteem. Sukracharya in Mahabharata reminds: "It is by their own actions, good or bad, that men are happy or miserable". Dhammapada adds: "If a man speaks acts with an evil thought, pain follows him, as the wheel follows the foot of the ox that draws the carriage"
4-3-1982.

❑ ❑ ❑ ❑ ❑

I think that the police must hold under its wings everything which is just, fair and human rights friendly. In that sense, every human being on earth is a policeman. Better to be a policeman than not to be. By being a good policeman, one may find peace in him and he can make peace for others.
27-10-1986.

❑ ❑ ❑ ❑ ❑

Every police station is public facility. But, how many policemen/officers accept it? It is felt by men and many others that the mental satisfaction people get in a police station is more important and efficacious than the merit of hundred decisions that ensure police justice to people. Be men of courteous behaviour and of perfect conduct. Honour everyone who comes to a police station. Good behaviour is a rare jewel.
3-3-1996.

❑ ❑ ❑ ❑ ❑

"A man should desire to be pleased with one who is superior to him in endowments; to be sympathetic towards one who is inferior in endowments, and seek friendliness with the one who is equal in endowments, doing thus he is not to be overcome by heart-burnings" (Srimad Bhagavata, Dhruvacharita). How is this in police? Think-think of it-always and every time. I found envy

and jealousy to anyone superior to another. People do not understand that "no man on earth hath envy raised to fame, while want of it hath driven none to shame" (Tirukkural).
17-11-1995.

❑ ❑ ❑ ❑ ❑

There are a number of posts created for top level officers-both inside and outside of the police department. Policemen ask: "Why the posts?" and they do not get an answer. Kautilya writes: "Whoever lessens the revenue eats the king's wealth; whoever doubles the revenue eats into the vitality of the country; whoever spends the revenue unproductively eats up the labour of the workmen". Is it true as far as the police are concerned?
14-12-1997.

❑ ❑ ❑ ❑ ❑

'Police is the friend of the people'-'A friend' in need is a friend indeed-And we are hearing such statements and wishful thinkings ever since we are born; yet we do not get people-friendly policemen. why? In Sanatsugatya, (V.13), it is written-"Six characteristics should be understood as belonging to friendship— that:

— one should rejoice at anything agreeable;
— feel grieved at anything disagreeable with a pure heart one;
— when asked by a deserving man, should give to him who asks what can certainly be given, though it may be beneficial to onself and even–though it ought not to be asked, namely one's favourites, sons, wealth.
— one should not dwell there where one has bestowed all one's wealth though a desire to get return for one's liberality.
— one should enjoy the fruit of one's own toils only,
— one should forgo one's own profit.

Policemen/officers must be told and taught about them when they enter the service.
24-11-1978.

❑ ❑ ❑ ❑ ❑

"Let our friendship be sincere with our brethren" (Rig Veda, 4,10,8) and I ask: 'How many policemen/officers think thus when they speak about police-public freindship. All may be a sort of publicity gymmick and therefore let every policeman/officer pray:" O Lord, the dispeller of darkness and remover of woe! Impart Thee that all beings may view me with a friendly eye and I may see them with lovely looks. May we all look at each other with a friendly eye". (Yajur Veda, 36, 18)
28-6-1988.

❑ ❑ ❑ ❑ ❑

Chanakya who said 'behaviour alone-it is that creates friends and foes'. I think that it is 100% true even today. If the police changed their behaviour and behavioural patterns when India got independence, perhaps the history of police for the last 50 years would have been altogether different today. Everyone, including police commissions, courts, researchers, people and the press, accuses police of undemocratic and unenviable behaviour.
18-10-1991.

❑ ❑ ❑ ❑ ❑

To me, justice is God, the truth, the love, the ethics, the fearlessness, the conscience, the aim in life — a policeman must think thus at least a hundred times in a day.
15-2-1990.

❑ ❑ ❑ ❑ ❑

What are the duties of policemen? They think that their duties are those which are conferred on them by law. Surely, they are their duties. But, they have more duties and Swamiji,

Vivekananda says: "Our duty to others means helping others, doing good to the world".
7-9-1987.

❑ ❑ ❑ ❑ ❑

Just listen to the cries of a man in police lockups. He has all the human rights which suspects may enjoy. A policeman/officer attains excellence if he looks at the detinue in a human rights friendly way. As regards his shape, he is just like a policeman/officer. He too has a father, a mother and many others. Law consists not in letters; it has a spirit. One who looks at people as human beings equal to others, he is said to be just and honest. Policeman ought to be just, honest and decent.

However much one may try, without people's willing co-operation and participation, nothing can be achieved in police work. In order to get the co-operation and participation, policemen/officers must—

1. have cool temper and should never utter unpleasant words (Uttradhain Sutra (1,8)
2. talk sweet and should have kindly looks and address others with pleasing words (Majh. Mohalla 1).
   19-9-1980.

"All the greatest discoveries of the world have been made without good equipment and under great difficulties-with nobody to encourage" (C.Rajagopalachari). Likewise, investigation of crime is 99 per cent persperation and 1 per cent luck or providence as you may call it " Bhageeratha's name has come to signify great preserverance in any good cause" (C.Rajagopalachari) and so is the case with all police works. I will be a successful policeman if I have perseverance and patience.
11-11-1983.

❑ ❑ ❑ ❑ ❑

How many police functionaries know what Longfellow said long ago-“we judge ourselves by what we feel capable of doing, while others judge us what we have already done”. What did the police do till now? The films, T.V. serials, press, research reports, reports of the police commissions and the people speak more about them than the policemen/officers. Listen to them-read them-reflect on them and decide the future course of action.
16-4-1987.

❑ ❑ ❑ ❑ ❑

“Action may not always brings happiness, but there is no happiness without action” (Disraeli). The police have to act and they have to do so justly, honestly and in a human rights friendly way. No doubt, such actions make them and the people happy.
13-1-1991.

❑ ❑ ❑ ❑ ❑

“The actions of men are the best interpreters of their thoughts”-said Locke. Police do a lot of things, but are they able to say that they do things in the right way?-with right thoughts? This is the problem. They feel it difficult to justify their thoughts and actions. P. Drucker once said:” It is more important to do the right thing than to do things right”.
17-3-1999.

❑ ❑ ❑ ❑ ❑

Why do policemen become angry and use third degree methods when they interrogate suspects? Many people ask this question and the policemen /officers have their ready-made answers to the question. The best answer is given by Haliburton. He says: “When a man is wrong and won't admit it, he always gets angry”. Is it not true?
10-7-1984.

❑ ❑ ❑ ❑ ❑

I have heard many police officers/men telling high about their superiors and I know why they do so. I see the same people

speak ill of them when they retire on superannuation. Why? Perhaps, Colton has an answer to it: "contemporaries appreciate the man rather than the merit: but posterity will regard the merit rather than the man".
23-10-1976.

❑ ❑ ❑ ❑ ❑

Police say that they have a lot of power and authority. But, many of them do not know what V.Mc Nabb speaks about power and authority. If so, just listen: "There are three theories of power and therefore of authority, to wit: the robber theory that all power is for mastery; the hireling theory that all power is for wealth; the good shepherd theory that all power is for service". For what do the police use their power and authority? There are many people who do not enjoy power and authority and for the police, they are poor. Yes, they are poor, for them the outlook is different. "Poverty wants some things, luxury, many avarices, all things' (Cowley) and if the policemen/officer has avarice, then he will certainly land in trouble. 27-7-1981.

❑ ❑ ❑ ❑ ❑

"A rose with all its sweetest leaves get folded"-Byron thought and I wish that every policeman/officer-even the director general of police-must have such thoughts always.
10-5-1978.

❑ ❑ ❑ ❑ ❑

I went to my superior and he said "but" to me-then I talked to my subordinates. They also said "but" and then I thought: "what 'buts? Everywhere 'buts' and everyone says "buts". Yes, then I heard Bulwer and I was told: "*But* is a word that cools a warm impulse, stifles many a kindly thought, puts a dead stop to many a brotherly deed. No one would ever love his neighbour as himself if he listened to all the *buts* that could be said".
20-2-1984.

❑ ❑ ❑ ❑ ❑

"Look at that officer, he is a womanizer! Look at this officer, he is a drunkard! Look at another officer, he is a divorcee! All of them are good administrators! They are just and honest! Why should we look at their private lives?"-some police officers/men say so often when they talk about others. They do not want to mix private life with their official life. For them, private life is different from public life-and-personal life different from official life. I do not agree with their views. For, I agree with Aeschines who said:" He who acts wickedly in private life can never be expected to show himself noble in public conduct. He that is base at home will not acquit himself with honour abroad, for it is not the man, but only the place that is changed".
24-11-1997.

❑ ❑ ❑ ❑ ❑

What is this? Some senior officers call constables :"boys' and I do not know what they mean by it. May be that the constables are '*treated as their children*' and if that is the case, the children need models. Joubert once said: "Children have more need of models than of critics". Are the senior ranks in police models to constable 'children'?
7-7-1977.

❑ ❑ ❑ ❑ ❑

'The civilization of police and policing' — this may be a new concept for Indian police. We want civilized policing and the "true test of civilization is not the census, nor the size of cities, nor the crops, but the kind of man that the Country turn out" — (Emerson). It goes, therefore, without saying that the true civilization of police and policing is not the strength of police, nor the power of police, nor the authority, nor the weapons, but the kind of policeman that the police service turns out.
1-3-1990.

❑ ❑ ❑ ❑ ❑

What is this? Everybody speaks about police in the west. They are decent, human rights friendly, considerate, just, prudent, people friendly and what not? This sort of argument irritates some police officers/men who do not want to hear the good sides of policing elsewhere. I do not think that they will improve in life. "People seldom improve when they have no other model but themselves to copy" (Goldsmith).
19-10-1989.

❑ ❑ ❑ ❑ ❑

Benjamin Disraeli says: "Circumstances are beyond the control of man; but his conduct is in his own power". The police too may realize that they can manage and manipulate their conduct whatever may be the circumstances under which they work. But, they must be prepared to enjoy or suffer the consequences of their action.
5-5-1998.

❑ ❑ ❑ ❑ ❑

For Cardinal Newman, "Conscience has rights because it has duties". For policeman, the law has conscience and he has to enforce law with a human conscience. After every act, examine the conscience. For, there is no witness so terrible, no accuser so powerful as conscience which dwells within us" (Sophocles). Police need to know more about human conscience, for, some of them lack it.

1. "Judge thyself with the judgement of sincerity, and thoug wilt judge others with the judgement of charity" (J.Mason)
2. "Good conscience is sometimes sold for money, but never brought with it" (Aughey)
3. "A man of integrity will never listen to any reason against conscience" (Home).

   2-2-1999.

❑ ❑ ❑ ❑ ❑

Police can be great if they want to be so. "Greatness lies not in being strong, but in the right using of strength" (H.W. Beecher).
6-6-1994.

❑ ❑ ❑ ❑ ❑

People speak of lawless law enforcement or what they call enforcement crimes. Enforcement crimes are numerous and the policemen know them more than others who suffer them. "Where the law ends, tyranny begins" (William Pitt) and that is what we must accept.
19-9-1998.

❑ ❑ ❑ ❑ ❑

People want 'equal justice' to all under law and procedure established by law. Are the police able to give criminal justice?-victim justice?-justice to society? There is a dispute about it. Justinian once said: "Justice is the constant desire and effort to render to every man his due". If that is so, do the police desire for the same? Do they make efforts for the same? Or, are they interested to give justice only to them? "Let justice be done though the world perishes" (Augustine of Hippo)
2-2-1993.

❑ ❑ ❑ ❑ ❑

How many policemen/officers are courageous enough to do justice? Waller says: "Of all virtues justice is the best; Valour without it is a common pest". I craved for justice to many. All of them guaranteed justice to me, but many did not have the boldness to be just to me.
12-2-1981.

❑ ❑ ❑ ❑ ❑

Are the police kind and considerate to the poor? the oppressed?-the downtrodden?-the weak?-the handicapped? Opinions differ, yet one may say with Bovee that "kindness is a

language the dumb can speak, the deaf can hear and understand". If that is so, why don't or cann't the policemen/ officers speak it? hear it? or understand it?
1-1-1995.

❑ ❑ ❑ ❑ ❑

I see policemen saluting their superiors. I see officers saluting their superiors. I see superiors reciprocating salutes. But, I doubt whether or not they give and receive salutes in the way they should and must. Manners are important in police, but some do not know that "manners require time, and nothing is more vulgar than haste" (Emerson). There is no loose salutes, watery salutes, ritualistic salutes. There is only *'salute'* in police and I see it only in limited occasions.
18-4-1995.

❑ ❑ ❑ ❑ ❑

"The heart has its reasons which reason does not know" (Pascal) and in interpersonnel relations, does heart have any place?
4-4-1994.

❑ ❑ ❑ ❑ ❑

'It is great to be great, but it is greater to be human" (W. Rogers). Human rights recognize no boundaries and all people have all human rights. Police have all human rights which any person has–nothing more, nothing less. People have great faith in police sense of human rights. Police can never extinguish human rights.
8-8-1998.

❑ ❑ ❑ ❑ ❑

I helped, in many ways, a superintendent of police to get some honours for him. He forgot it and started to persecute me. He was certainly ungrateful to me. He did not know that :

"Ingratitude is treason to mankind" (Thompson). Or was he a man of no values? Let him remember: Ingratitude "thrives too fast at first but fades in time" (Sir Samuel Garth).
7-1-1989.

❑ ❑ ❑ ❑ ❑

G.K. Chesterton once said: "A dead thing can go with the stream, but only a living thing can go against it". Surely, that is true? Then a question-i.e. what type of policeman/officer goes after a politician? A policeman/officer who lives like a policeman/officer never goes with or after a politician. If his life is a burden, he bears it-if it is a duty, he dares it.
31-10-1981.

❑ ❑ ❑ ❑ ❑

"Life is like an onion; you peel it off one layer at a time, and sometimes you weep" (C.Sandnurg) and police life is no exception to this general rule.
15-5-1984.

❑ ❑ ❑ ❑ ❑

Police is a man-oriented service and everywhere man comes at the center. Policeman must therefore realize that "man is the perfection of the creation" (Chandogya Upanishad, 2-6-1). If he does so, certainly there may not be any human rights violations in police custody. G.K. Chesterton says that "man is not merely an evolution, but rather a revolution". Yes, he is and surely, every man is born with dignity and must be treated with dignity. But, he is really a wonder!

> "As a rule, man is a fool;
> When it's hot, he wants it cool,
> When it's cool, he wants it hot,
> Always wanting what is not!" (Anon)

29-6-1988.

❑ ❑ ❑ ❑ ❑

"Civility costs nothing, but buys everything" (Lady M.W. Montague). "What is the need for using filthy expressions and foul words during police-citizen interactions.
31-7-1986.

❑ ❑ ❑ ❑ ❑

"Manners make the man" (Daniel Defoe) and policeman too.
21-10-1992

❑ ❑ ❑ ❑ ❑

In police, inservice courses are sparingly conducted and all do not attend them. Courses on human relations, police citizens interactions, gender justice, juvenile justice, victim justice, equal justice etc. are rarely organized for all and many senior levels are as ignorant as the juniors in this aspect. What to do to convince the administration about the need for inservice training ? "The mind is like a clock that is constantly running down; it has to be wound up daily with good thoughts" (Fulton J.Sheen). If that is the reality, the higher and highest echelons in the hierarchy need periodical inservice training courses.
11-9-1990.

❑ ❑ ❑ ❑ ❑

Corrupt men may realize that "money is a good servant but a poor master". It has destroyed many policemen/officers and shown the way to jails/imprisoned them. that is the reason why Fielding said : "Make money your god, it will plague you like the devil".
7-11-1998.

❑ ❑ ❑ ❑ ❑

There can be no policing without morality and no morality without policing — the self, others and society. Emerson says : "There can be no high civility without morality".
19-4-1992.

❑ ❑ ❑ ❑ ❑

"Noice proves nothing. Often a hen who merely laid an egg cackles as if she had laid an asteroid"(Mark Twain). Likewise, some policemen officers make noice wherever they go.
10-10-1991

❑ ❑ ❑ ❑ ❑

I have heard some policemen/officers shouting at others. Sound pollution indeed! Why ? I do not know. They shout at others as they are the parade commanders. They shout at people- at subordinates. They do not do it with politicians. Why? They shout at people who are afraid of them. They fail to understand that shouting to make people obey is like driving the car with the horn. What a tragedy indeed!
27-3-1990.

❑ ❑ ❑ ❑ ❑

Some policemen/officers admit that they are hot-tampered. Why? what do they do to put it down ? Realization of one's weakness is a blessing. They can correct it if they want so. But they do not do so. They do not get peace of mind. "True quietness of heart is won by resisting our passions, not by obeying them".(Thomas a Kempis).
1-11-1991.

❑ ❑ ❑ ❑ ❑

The director general of police asked me today: "what is your message to the third millennium police?".

J.C.Mitchell said :

"Perhaps you can not be a star.
But you need not be cloud".
Edward Everett Hale said :
"Look up and not down;
Out and not in ;
Forward and not back;
And lend a hand".

And certainly they did not give a message to the police. Hence I said: "Have optimism-and-be an optimist. There is always a better way to do things-and strive for it-and you will reach there-the Omega in policing".
31-12-1999

❑ ❑ ❑ ❑ ❑

Albert Einstein was a genius and he said : "Sometimes one pays most for things one gets for nothing". And the people in a democracy pay heavily for maintaining police-for getting some service from police-even for getting something which people get nothing.
2-5-1986.

❑ ❑ ❑ ❑ ❑

Many policemen/officers ask the politicians : "What to do? How to go about ?"-this is an allegation often heard against police. People say that the police listen to politicians more than to their patrons in a democracy-the police patrons in a democracy are the people, the tax-payers. Patrons complain that the politicians can not believe what the police do for them or on their behalf. They disbelieve their eyes and ears. Charles De Gaulle once said: "Since a politician never believes what he says, he is surprised when others believe him". Is it true in police as well?
27-9-1983.

❑ ❑ ❑ ❑ ❑

Just listen to K.Hubbard : "If there's anything a public servant hates to do, it is something for the public". Is it true to say so about the .police ?
18-8-1989.

❑ ❑ ❑ ❑ ❑

People will be better if the police change their attitude-say the people:

Debate is going on for decades.

Dispute is going on without solutions

Quarrelling is continuing......

and

"Quarrels would never last if fault was only on one side" (La Rochefoucauld)
17-10-1985.

❑ ❑ ❑ ❑ ❑

Filthy language irritates all-no matter, from whom it comes.

"The tongue breaketh bone

Though itself has none" (Anon).

People say that epithets and indecent expressions are a part of police culture. The policemen/officers do not understand: "A slip of the foot you may soon recover,

But a slip of the tongue you may never get over (Franklin)

If policemen speak in sober language, perhaps police-citizen relationship would have been altogether different today.
19-9-1979.

❑ ❑ ❑ ❑ ❑

"By examining the tongue, physicians find out the diseases of the body; and philosophers, the diseases of the mind and heart (Justine). In police, by examining the tongue, one may understand the culture of the service. No bullet penetrates so deeply and fiercely as an evil police tongue.
1-12-1998.

❑ ❑ ❑ ❑ ❑

Politicians speak a lot about justice.

Policemen too.

"All bow to virtue, and then walk away" (De Finod)

18-10-1978.

❑ ❑ ❑ ❑ ❑

Policemen-the constables-complain of their dissatisfaction-salary-wise, status-wise, and satisfaction-wise

What to do ?

No doubt, they affect police-citizen interactions 16-1-1978

❑ ❑ ❑ ❑ ❑

"There are four things a woman needs to know"-says Mrs. Caroline Simon. And they are—

"How to look like a girl;
Act like a lady;
Think like a man and
Work like a dog".

Likewise, there are four or five things a policeman needs to know , And they are—

How to look like a gentleman;
Speak like a gentleman
Act like a gentleman
Think like a gentleman and
Work like a gentleman

A policeman is a man, but every man is not a gentleman. 14-6-1986.

❑ ❑ ❑ ❑ ❑

Anon says—

"Do your best and leave the rest
What is the use of crying?
Firm endeavour stands the test
More than haste or hurry.
Rich rewards will come to him,
Who work on with smiling vim".

10-10-1990.

❑ ❑ ❑ ❑ ❑

I want to pray once again and always:-

"From the unreal, lead me to the real,

From the darkness, lead me to light,

From death, lead me to immortality"

and that is what Brihad Upanishad tells us.
31-12-1999.

❑ ❑ ❑ ❑ ❑

Every policeman writes a diary and if one is able to read a few, he will be able to know many things about the police and policing a society. Nobody reads another man's diary in police and therefore, I thought: "let people read a few of my thoughts in my diary''. I have written a lot in my diary, but a few day's jottings were reproduced. I wrote a book "Management Thoughts on Police Administration" and it gives more of my thoughts. Why I am not a Policeman ? I have thought about it several times and certainly, I am a Policeman — one among them and none among them.

Bibliography

Arnold, David, *The Police and Colonial Control in South India*, Social Scientist, July, 1976.

Bhardwaj, R.K., *Indian Police Administration*, National, New Delhi, 1978.

Blum, Richard, H. *Police Selection,* Charles C. Thomas, Springfield, 1964.

Bopp, W. J., *Police Administration: Selected Readings*, Holbrook Press, Boston, 1975.

Bose, A.C., *Police Indiscipline and Police*, Amrita Bazar Patrika, 9, September, 1969.

Bowes, Stuart, *Police and Civil Liberties*, Lawrence & Wishart, London, 1966.

Clift, Raymond, E., *A Guide to Modern Police Thinking: An Introduction to Policing*, 3rd ed., W.H. Anderson, Cincinnati, 1970.

Curry, J. C., *The Indian Police*, Faber & Faber London, 1932.

Elliott, J. F., *New Police*, Charles C. Thomas, Springfield, 1973.

Elmen, Frank, *The Police As A Career*, Batsford, London, 1962.

Franser, Lord, *The Police in the Judicial Process*, Police Journal, October-December, 1972.

Frost, Thomas, M., *A Forward Look in Police Education*, Charles C. Thomas Springfield, 1959.

Fry, J.E., *Police in Fact and Fiction*, Police Journal, Dec. 1963

Hart, J.M., *British Police*, Allen & Unwin, London, 1951.

Hewitt, William, H., *British Police Administration*, Charles C. Thomas, Springfield, 1965.

Iannone, N.F., *Supervision of Police Personnel*, 2nd ed., Prentice Hall, Englewood Cliffs, 1975.

Iyenger, H.V.R., *Use and Abuse of Police Power*, Indian Express, 18, April, 1968.

Jacob, Ian, *The Future of the Police*, Police Journal, July, 1967.

Kenney, John P., *Police Management Planining*, Charles C. Thomas, Springfield, 1959.

Kenney, John P., *Team Policing Organization:A Theoretical Model*, Police, August, 1972.

Kooken, Don L., *Ethics in Police Service*, Charles C. Thomas, Springfield, 1957.

Kripalani, J.B., *Our Police During the Emergency*, Indian Express, 31 May 1977.

Lahiri, B.N., *Dilemma of thePolice*, Indian Police Journal, July-September, 1968.

Leonard, V.A. *Police Organization and Management*, 2nd ed., Foundation Press, Brooklyn, 1964.

Lewis, Roy, E., *Force for the Future*, Temple-Smith, London, 1976.

Macnamara, Donald, E.J. and Mare Reidel (eds), *Police: Perpectives, Problems, Prospects*, Prager, New York, 1974.

Mark, Robert, *Policing a Perplexed Society*, Allen & Unwin, London, 1977.

Meynell, Laurence, *Policeman in the Family*, Oxford University Press, London 1953.

Mitra, Dilip, *Indian Police Today*, SVP Magazine, November, 1977.

Modak, S.C., *Our Police,* Illustrated Weekly of India, 12, December, 1971.

Mukherjee, Dilip, *Police and Politicians*, Times of India, 7, August 1969.

Murray, Joseph A., *Police Administration and Criminal Investigation*, 3rd ed., Arco, New York, 1968.

Nayar, Kuldip, *Role of Police*, Indian Express, 29, July, 1976.

Noorani, A.G., *Police Excesses: Need For Institutional Safeguards*, Indian Express, 9, March 1976.

Pell, Arthur, R., *Police Leadership*, Charles C. Thomas, Springfield, 1967.

Reith, Charles, *British Police and Democratic Ideal*, Oxford University Press, London, 1943.

Saksena, N.S., *Neglect of Police Stations,* CBI Bulletin, June, 1976.

Sastri, B.S., *Planning for Law and Order*, SVP NPA Magazine, July, 1976.

Scott, H., *Police Problems of Today*, Stevens, London, 1949

Shanti, Prasad, *Towards a New Police*, Indian Police Journal, July, 1964.

Shur, E.M., *Crime Without Victims*, Prentice Hall, Englewood Cliffs, 1965.

Singhvi, G.C. *National Planning and Police*, Indian Journal of Public Administration, October-December 1971.

Sinha, M.K., *Reforms in Police Administration*, Indian Police Journal, October, 1961.

Stretcher, V.C., *The Environment of Law Enforcement*, Prentice Hall, Englewood Cliffs, 1971.

Thomas, J.L., *Police Administration*, Police Review, London, 1953.

Trikha, M.C., *The British Police At Work* , Police Research and Development, January-June, 1974.

Vadackumchery, James, *Indian Police and Equal Justice Under Law*, A.P.H. Publishing Corporation, Delhi, 1999.

Vadackumchery, James, *Police Leadership:The Inside Story*, A.P.H. Publishing Corporation, Delhi, 1999.

Vadackumchery, James, *Third Millennium Police: Take Off Trends in India*, A.P.H. Publishing Corporation, Delhi, 2000.

Varghese, A., *Constables: Our Weakest Link*, NPA Magazine, November 1972.

Verma, Upendra, *SHO and the Indian Police*, Indian Police Journal, January-March, 1976.

Wilson, O.W. and Roy, C. McLaren, *Police Administration*, 4th ed., McGraw Hills, New York, 1977.

Wright, R.Gene and Jone A. Marls, *The Police Officer and the Criminal Justice*, McGraw Hills, New York, 1970.

❑❑❑

Index

❑❑❑